From Welcomed Exiles to Illegal Immigrants

From Welcomed Exiles to Illegal Immigrants

Cuban Migration to the U.S., 1959–1995

by
Felix Roberto Masud-Piloto

ROWMAN & LITTLEFIELD PUBLISHERS, INC.

ROWMAN & LITTLEFIELD PUBLISHERS, INC.

Published in the United States of America
by Rowman & Littlefield Publishers, Inc.
4720 Boston Way, Lanham, Maryland 20706

3 Henrietta Street
London WC2E 8LU, England

British Cataloging in Publication Information Available

Library of Congress Cataloging-in-Publication Data
Masud-Piloto, Felix Roberto.
From welcomed exiles to illegal immigrants : Cuban migration
to the U.S., 1959–1995 / by Felix Roberto Masud-Piloto.
p.   cm.
Includes bibliographical references and index.
1. Refugees, Political—Florida—History.   2. Refugees, Political
—United States—History.   3. Refugees, Political—Cuba—History.
4. United States—Foreign relations—Cuba.   5. Cuba—Foreign
relations—United States.   6. Cubans—Florida—History.   7. United
States—Emigration and immigration—History.   I. Title.
HV640.5.C9M35   1995   304.8'7307291—dc20   95-25772

ISBN 0-8476-8148-3 (cloth : alk. paper)
ISBN 0-8476-8149-1 (pbk. : alk. paper)

Printed in the United States of America

⊗™The paper used in this publication meets the minimum requirements of
American National Standard for Information Sciences—Permanence of
Paper for Printed Library Materials, ANSI Z39.48-1984.

A la memoria de mis padres Félix Masud y Victoria Piloto
que fueron, son, y serán siempre mis guías.

Contents

Contents

Tables

Contents ix

Foreword

LIKE MOST GOOD BOOKS, this volume is written from the heart
and from the mind. In his moving introduction, Professor Masud-
Piloto, a young Cuban historian, tells how exile affected his family
and himself. Although the author's central theme is the political
manipulation of the Cuban exile drama by the governments of
Cuba and the United States, he constantly reminds us of the hopes
and fears, achievements and frustrations of displaced Cubans. The
story of Roberto Ramírez (a pseudonym) in Chapter 7 reminds us
how momentous events of international struggles reflect themselves in individual human lives. For Professor Masud-Piloto, this
scholarly study is part of a long, deeply personal struggle to
understand the divided historical paths of his fellow Cubans. His
love for all the Cuban people—in the Cuban community abroad
and in Cuba—is manifest in his book.

Dispassionate analysis of the Cuban revolution is rare: sadly it
seems easier to praise angels and damn devils than to understand
real people in history. Given his heartfelt commitment to the
subject, therefore, it is remarkable that the author has achieved a
high degree of balance and judicious historical perspective. He
recognizes that the Cuban migration since 1959 can only be
understood in terms of a long prior history that included earlier
migrations to the United States. Those earlier migrations also
stemmed from political upheaval and economic distress. Revolutionary sentiment existed in Cuba from the early nineteenth
century, intensified in the patriotic anti-colonial cause against
Spain which began in 1868, and ended in frustration with the U.S.
intervention of 1898. (Textbooks in the United States refer to the
"Spanish-American War" as if Cubans had not fought and died for
thirty years in their own war of national liberation, as if Cubans

had no significant presence in their own history.) As has been documented in countless histories, between 1898 and 1958 the United States played a dominating and decisive role in Cuba, frustrating the widespread nationalist desire for political, economic, and cultural liberation until 1959. Nationalism, not "communism," was and is the strongest current of anti–United States feeling in Cuba. In Cuba, as in Nicaragua, repeated U.S. intervention helped intensify nationalism and breed revolution. Those who would understand more recent chapters in Cuban history—such as the one recounted herein—would do well to reflect on earlier events for which the United States, seemingly afflicted with selective historical amnesia in recent years, cannot escape responsibility.

Arguably, the most important process of the half-millennium of world history since Columbus has been that controversial phenomenon "imperialism," or as its apologists call it, "the expansion of Western Civilization." Also arguably, the most important trend of the twentieth century has been the nationalistic struggle against "imperialism" by the peoples of the Third World. Non-violent campaigns and wars for national liberation have swept Latin America and the Caribbean, Africa, and Asia, changing the global map, the character of the United Nations, and to some small extent power relations between rich and poor nations. Professor Masud-Piloto locates his story in the context of the Cold War, perceived by many as essentially an East-West struggle of superpowers. The Cold War also involves relations between rich and/or powerful superpowers of the "North" and poor countries of the "South" (the Third World). The United States's Cold War foreign policy—the Containment Policy—was not designed only to contain the Soviet Union, but also to frustrate the aspirations of the people of the "South" as well. George Kennan, head of planning of the U.S. Department of State, an architect of the Containment Policy, noted in a secret memorandum in 1948:

> We have about 50% of the world's wealth, but only 6.3% of its population. . . . In this situation, we cannot fail to be object of envy and resentment. Our real task in the coming period is to devise a pattern of relationships which will permit us to maintain this position of disparity without positive detriment to our national security. To do so, we will have to dispense with all sentimentality and day-dreaming; and our attention will have to be concentrated

everywhere on our immediate national objectives. We need not deceive ourselves that we can afford today the luxury of altruism and world-benefaction. . . . We should cease to talk about vague . . . unreal objectives such as human rights, the raising of living standards, and democratization. The day is not far off when we are going to have to deal in straight power concepts. The less we are then hampered by idealistic slogans, the better.*

The Cuban revolution was a vigorous challenge to the North-South Containment Policy. In response the United States adopted Kennan's "straight power concepts." But "idealistic slogans," far from being abandoned, were retained to cloak and to legitimize United States policies, as the "Open Arms," "Freedom Flights," and "Freedom Flotilla" of this study bear witness.

In his revealing chapter contrasting U.S. policy toward Cuban migrants with its policies toward refugees from rightist regimes in Haiti and Central America, Professor Masud-Piloto lays bare the contradictions and hypocrisy that threaten to overwhelm and defeat the strain of genuine humanitarianism in U.S. immigration policy. The Cuban migrant stream since 1959 has been joined by a strong current from anti-communist regimes in the hemisphere; both have united with a broad historical tide pulled by the wealth of the United States and pushed by Caribbean Basin poverty. One poll in friendly, "democratic," tourist-paradise, English-speaking Jamaica showed that an astonishing 60 percent of Jamaicans would emigrate to the United States if they could!† Thus while welcoming refugees "fleeing communism," the United States has attempted to erect stern barriers against those who try to escape poverty and repression in nominally capitalist, nominally pro–United States nations. In 1981 I heard, in a public lecture, an obviously embarrassed Deputy Assistant Secretary of State of Hispanic descent twice affirm that the United States had created "concentration camps" in south Florida to discourage Haitian boat people.

The Cuban government has also played politics with refugees and political prisoners, as Professor Masud-Piloto makes clear. It has used exile to rid the revolution of enemies, dissenters, noncon-

*E. Bradford Burns, *At War in Nicaragua: The Reagan Doctrine and the Politics of Nostalgia* (New York: Harper & Row, 1987), pp. 17–18, quoting Thomas Etzold and John Lewis Gaddis, *Containment* (New York: Columbia Univ. Press, 1978), pp. 226–27.
†Carl Stone, *The Political Opinions of the Jamaican People (1976–81)* (Kingston, Jamaica: Blackett, 1982), 64.

formists, sociopaths, and those who simply tire of austerity and sacrifice in what remains a poor Third World country living cheek-by-jowl with the flashy glitter of south Florida. As the almost-Greek tragedy of U.S.–Cuban relations recycles blinded and outworn power concepts and Cold War ideological sloganeering, neither the United States nor Cuba wins, but the divided people on both sides of the Florida Straits lose.

New Camariocas and new Mariels are possible. The prospect also exists of a new Fortress America, sternly armed to reject not simply "communism," but also millions of Haitians, Dominicans, Jamaicans, Mexicans, Guatemalans, Salvadorans, Nicaraguans, and others who hope to escape social upheaval, poverty, and persecution.

To avoid this grim scenario, two things must happen. In the long term, the United States must allow the people of the Caribbean and Central America to solve the problems of poverty, social injustice, and underdevelopment *in their own ways, based on their own intimate knowledge of their histories and societies.* In the short term, as Professor Masud-Piloto argues in the conclusion of his valuable study, the United States (working in equal partnership with neighboring countries and heeding its best instincts as expressed in the church-based Sanctuary Movement) must end the contradictions, hypocrisies, uncertainties, and brutalities of current refugee policies. As the author notes, "it is time for the United States to adopt a single, non-ideological, humanitarian standard for granting refugee status." With this book, Professor Masud-Piloto has contributed directly to a worthy goal that could save perhaps millions of people from unnecessary suffering.

Darrell E. Levi
Florida State University

Preface

OVER THIRTY-THREE YEARS have passed since my father and I left Cuba with a mixture of sadness, anxiety, and hope. Although our departure, like most others during the period, was clouded in fear and seeming urgency, we felt confident of a successful outcome. My parents, like thousands of others, were certain that the revolution would last only a few months or at the most a few years. Thus they decided to emigrate to wait for political changes in Cuba.

My father, who was forty-nine years old at the time, was at the peak of his career in Cuba and had much to lose if our stay in the United States were to be prolonged. He was considered a sort of "Cuban success story." Coming to Cuba as an eight-year-old immigrant from Beirut, Lebanon, in 1920, he rose from poverty to fame and relative wealth in a few years. His highly successful and visible career as a popular trainer of boxers and baseball players made him well known in sports, political, and show-business circles. He had traveled widely with boxing champions and baseball teams. Yet he decided to risk fame and stability for the uncertainty of exile.

Years later I discovered that I had been the principal reason for my family's exile. Impressed by rumors making the rounds in Cuba, my parents, and many others with young children, became worried. My parents were fearful that I would soon be indoctrinated by the new socialist government and eventually be inducted into the army to defend the revolution. I was ten years old then and oblivious to the dangers my parents foresaw. In fact, I was quite excited by the atmosphere of change brought on by the revolution. Batista's overthrow, Castro's triumphant march into Havana, the literacy campaign, the agrarian and urban reforms, the explosion of *La Coubre* in Havana Harbor, the "El Encanto" burning, and the Bay of Pigs invasion were still vivid in my mind when I said goodbye to dear friends, my three sisters, and my mother.

On October 15, 1961, a small number of Cuban friends greeted us at Miami's International Airport with the often-heard phrase: "We'll be back in Cuba in six months." One of our friends even insisted that I go live with his family for that short period to avoid extra expense. My father declined the offer.

Our first few weeks in Miami were spent anxiously awaiting news from Cuba of Castro's "certain" downfall. I took the period as an extended vacation, missing home but confident that I would soon return. Six months passed and Castro's power grew stronger. Instead of returning to Cuba, we were joined by my mother and two sisters in 1962. By the time my other sister joined us in Miami in 1969, a deep sense of permanency had set in.

Compared to thousands of other Cuban families, our immediate family was reunited rather quickly, and slowly the rest of our extended family joined the constantly growing Cuban community in Miami. Two paternal uncles arrived with their families in the late 1960s; a maternal aunt arrived via Madrid in the early 1970s. Most recently, the Mariel boatlift brought us twelve relatives: a paternal aunt, three cousins, and their families. Yet we still have relatives in Cuba whom most of our family in Miami have not seen in more than thirty years.

Life in exile has been difficult for all of us, but particularly for our parents. My father never regained the status he enjoyed in Cuba. Nor was he ever able to practice his profession, since to do so he needed to pass a revalidation examination offered only in English, which he never learned. Like thousands of other exiled professionals, he worked at menial jobs to survive and provide for his family. He died in Miami at the age of eighty-one, still dreaming of returning to the "old" Cuba.

My mother, Victoria, although always a lively and robust woman, was simply overwhelmed by Cuban political events of the late 1950s and early 1960s. The constant turmoil, family separation, and the imprisonment of a brother and sister (Leonel was sentenced to twenty years and Emilia to fifteen) affected her deeply. By the time she came to Miami in 1962, she was suffering from hypertension and was often ill with related ailments. Mother never felt at home in Miami. She constantly missed Cuba and her loved ones, especially her brother and sister in prison. Emilia was released after serving six years of her sentence, and she joined us in Miami a few months later. Mother never saw Leonel again; he died in Cuba just a few months after serving his twenty-year term.

After a long illness mother passed away in a Miami hospital on January 23, 1984. Like tens of thousands of other Cubans, she died dreaming of going back to Cuba to her familiar surroundings, to what she had left, presumably for just a few months, almost twenty-two years earlier.

October 15, 1961, will remain in my mind as the day I unsuspectingly started a new life in a foreign country where everything, including the language, was unknown to me. Sad and difficult as I found it, I was not alone; almost one million Cubans have faced similar circumstances since 1959. Since then I have searched for answers to the fundamental questions of how and why this massive migration took place. I hope this extremely brief history of my family's experience will have shed some light and provided some perspective for understanding the following pages.

About the Sources

Any analysis of the Cuban migration to the United States must begin with an exploration of its roots, causes, and circumstances. Despite its historical significance, however, the Cuban migration of 1959–1995 has been largely ignored by historians. Most published works on the period have been produced by sociologists, social workers, political scientists, economists, and psychologists. I have benefited greatly from their work and drawn extensively from it.

Much of the data for this work comes from primary documents available in Cuba and the United States, namely newspapers, periodicals, and private and public documents relating to some of the key participants. I have used those sources whenever possible with the hopes of providing some understanding of the political maneuvers that took place behind the scenes and how they affected the refugees.

Unfortunately, much of the material on the Cuban migration in the Presidential Libraries is still classified and unavailable to researchers. I have requested the declassification of over two hundred pages of documents, but the process has been extremely slow and not very fruitful. As of this writing, I have been successful in the declassification of only twelve pages. I have been rejected for over one hundred pages, and have not received word on another eighty. I hope that when those materials become available, other researchers will be able to improve on this study.

Research for this work has taken me to places I never imagined visiting: Abilene, Kansas, where the Dwight D. Eisenhower Presidential Library is located, and Austin, Texas, site of the Lyndon B. Johnson Presidential Library. Other more familiar places fruitful to my research were the John F. Kennedy Presidential Library in Boston, Massachusetts; Miami, Florida; and Havana, Cuba, where I was able to interview people who played a role in my own emigration. I was also fortunate to work in the Latin American collections of the universities of Florida, Texas, and Miami, and Harvard University, where I found a number of valuable materials.

In addition to scholarly works, I have also incorporated the views of family members and friends through a number of random interviews conducted in Havana and Miami from 1979 to 1985. While those interviews do not represent a scientific sampling, they provide a more direct human perspective on the migration's effects on both participants and observers. The case of Nilda Baró, a close family friend and our closest neighbor in Cuba, is a good example. Talking to Nilda after almost two decades of separation provided an in-depth perspective not available in any library in the world. Equally valuable were my interviews and visits with Asdrubal Baró, Nilda's son and a childhood friend of mine. Being able to compare and contrast our lives since 1961 and to discuss our perceptions of the United States, the revolution, and ourselves was a priceless experience, one that unfortunately not all exiles will have.

I do not use the interviews extensively, but I feel they should be mentioned as part of this work because, despite its predominantly political character, the Cuban migration has been and remains a deeply personal and emotional experience for all Cubans.

About the Cover

THE PHOTOGRAPH THAT APPEARS on the cover of this book was taken off the coast of Cojímar, Cuba, in August 1994. It shows the faces of anonymous men as they risked their lives at sea—on anything that floated—in a desperate attempt to make it to the coast of southern Florida. They were trying to do what tens of thousands of Cubans had done since 1959. They expected, like their precursors, to be received as heroes and welcomed in the United States with open arms and open hearts.

For 32,000 "balseros" (rafters) of the more than 35,000 who attempted to reach U.S. shores in 1994, a very different destiny awaited. On August 19, 1994, President Bill Clinton closed the doors that had been opened to Cubans for more than thirty-five years. From that day on, Cubans were intercepted at sea and transported to detention camps at the U.S. Naval Station at Guantánamo Bay, Cuba. At the time of this writing (September 1995), more than 12,000 rafters remain in detention at Guantánamo, after several thousand were admitted to the United States on humanitarian grounds: unaccompanied children, those over 70 years of age and their guardians, and the gravely ill. Hundreds of others, out of frustration and depression, have returned to Cuba, and a few have lost their lives either by suicide or trying to escape what most of them call concentration camps.

The plight of the rafters added high drama and tragedy to the long history of the Cuban migration to the United States. In addition to the 32,000 who braved the poor living conditions at Guantánamo, hundreds are believed to have died at sea during the summer of 1994. According to conservative estimates, out of every four rafters who attempted the passage, one died trying.

I don't know if the men who grace the cover of this book were rescued at sea and transported to Guantánamo, or if they lost their lives trying to cross the Florida Straits. I only hope that this work, and all my work on the Cuban migration to the United States, contributes to a better understanding of this human tragedy.

Acknowledgments

MUCH HAS HAPPENED in the ongoing story of the Cuban migration to the United States since the publication of *With Open Arms* in 1988. In fact, the reversals in U.S. policy have forced me to change the title of this revised and expanded edition to *From Welcomed Exiles to Illegal Immigrants*. I feel that this title reflects more accurately the evolution of and contradictions in U.S. policy. The changes in policy have made my work more challenging as I continue trying to document as much of this fascinating human story as possible. Such a task would have been impossible without the help, support, encouragement, and advice of my family, many good friends, and colleagues.

First and foremost, I would like to recognize and thank my family, beginning with my wife María Dolores. She has been involved in every aspect of this project, and most importantly, provided the necessary encouragement and kindness during difficult moments. My sisters Nancy, Emilia, and María de los Angeles provided valuable information about our family's migration. They have always supported my work, despite its controversial nature, and even when we held radically different political opinions.

I am extremely grateful to Darrell Levi for being a great teacher and a true friend. His foreword to the first edition is reprinted in its entirety and without revisions; it is as relevant today as it was in 1988.

Since 1988 I have made five research trips to Cuba, where I have had the good fortune of working with a group of young researchers who have provided important information and perspective to my work. Chief among them is Ernesto Rodríguez Chávez of the Centro de Estudios Sobre América. Ernesto has been an invaluable source of information, statistics, and photographs. I am also most

grateful to my Cuban colleagues Mercedes Arce, Milagros Martínez, Rafael Hernández, Jorge Hernández, Consuelo Martín, and
Antonio Aja, for their valuable and unselfish contributions to my
work.

I would also like to thank Louis A. Pérez, Gerald Poyo, Lázaro
Verdías, Juan Manuel Macho, Jorge Riquelme, Héctor Vélez, and
Mary Jo Dudley. Their support, suggestions, and criticism have
made this a better work.

My work has greatly benefited from the efforts and support of
my staff at DePaul University's Center for Latino Research: Mer-
vin Méndez, Yolanda Quiñones, Susana Ochoa and María de los
Angeles Corral provided most of the technical support I needed to
complete the manuscript. Also at DePaul, Marisa Alicea, José
Solís, Rose Spalding, and Mirza González have encouraged and supported my work.

Last, but certainly not least, I am most grateful to Rowman &
Littlefield for having faith in my work and giving me an opportunity to revise and expand this study. Special thanks go to Jennifer
Ruark for her confidence in me, her patience with, and her understanding of, my delays in delivering the manuscript.

I am eternally grateful to the individuals listed above. Their suggestions, advice, and criticisms have greatly improved my research
and provided me with a deeper understanding of the Cuban migration to the United States.

From Welcomed Exiles to Illegal Immigrants

Cuban Migration to the United States, 1959–1980

Year	Number
1959[a]	26,527
1960[b]	60,224
1961	49,961
1962	78,611
1963	42,929
1964	15,616
1965	16,447
1966	46,688
1967	52,147
1968	55,945
1969	52,625
1970	49,545
1971	50,001
1972	23,977
1973	12,579
1974	13,670
1975	8,488
1976	4,515
1977[c]	4,548
1978	4,108
1979	2,644
1980	122,061
Total, January 1, 1959, to September 30, 1980	793,856
Total, April 1, 1980, to December 31, 1980	125,118

[a] For 1959 the figures are for January 1 to June 30.

[b] For 1960 through 1976 the figures are for fiscal years beginning July 1 and ending June 30.

[c] For 1977 through 1980 the figures are for fiscal years beginning October 1 and ending September 30.

Source: Sergio Díaz Briquets and Lisandro Pérez, *Cuba: The Demography of Revolution* (Washington, D.C.: Population Reference Bureau, vol. 36, no. 1, April 1981), p. 26. Reprinted with permission from Thomas D. Boswell and James R. Curtis, *The Cuban-American Experience: Culture, Images and Perspectives* (Totowa, N.J.: Rowman and Allanheld, 1984), 42.

Introduction

ON AUGUST 19, 1994, PRESIDENT BILL CLINTON, following a precedent set by most of his last eight predecessors, used his executive powers to stop an uncontrolled migration from Cuba. On that day, the president reversed the thirty-five-year-old practice of welcoming with open arms Cubans "escaping" Fidel Castro's regime. Instead he instituted a closed-door policy designed to intercept hopeful refugees at sea and transport them to detention camps at the U.S. Naval Base at Guantánamo Bay, Cuba. According to the new regulations, those rescued at sea faced indefinite detention in the base, and would not be allowed to plead their cases for political asylum in the United States. Thus, overnight, Cubans who had come to believe that immigrating to the United States was their natural right found themselves no longer welcome in this country.

The president's decision marked the first time since the end of World War II that the United States denied political asylum to people fleeing a Communist government. The policy reversal was even more startling in light of the fact that in 1994 Cuba was among only a handful of Communist governments left in the world, and the only one with which the United States had consistently refused to reach any form of accommodation. The United States did not hesitate to negotiate with and normalize its relations with the Communist governments of China, Vietnam, and North Korea, but pledged to continue its hardline policy of economic strangulation toward Havana until Castro accepted U.S. demands for political changes in Cuba that would lead to the end of his Communist government.

This study analyzes the political dynamics at work during the migration of more than one million Cubans to the United States from 1959 to 1995. The main questions addressed are those concerning the reasons, motivations, and circumstances for the migration. It does not pretend to tell the story of the Cuban exile community, nor to measure the success or failure of that community in the United States; such an endeavor would require a much wider and more extensive work than this.

Particular emphasis has been placed on the unusual events and the contradictions that have made the migration in many ways unique: the Cuban [unaccompanied] Children's Program, the Camarioca boatlift, the Cuban airlift, the Mariel boatlift, and the exodus of 32,000 "rafters" during the summer of 1994. Because of the migration's political nature, the following events affecting Cuba–United States relations are also discussed at some length: the Cold War, the Bay of Pigs invasion, and the dialogue between the Cuban government and the exile community.

The Cuban migration was triggered primarily by complex revolutionary changes in Cuba and the United States' response to such changes, which included, among other measures, encouraging the migration. In addition to ostensibly humanitarian reasons, every administration from Dwight Eisenhower's to Bill Clinton's has, in one way or another, welcomed refugees from Cuba in order to further political objectives against the revolution. Although those objectives have varied during the past thirty-six years, at least two have remained constant: (a) to destabilize Castro's government by draining it of vital human resources (such as physicians, teachers, and technicians); and (b) to discredit the regime through encouraging the flight of thousands from a Communist dictatorship to a capitalist democracy.

Intransigent U.S. opposition to the Cuban revolution gave refugees from that country characteristics that set them apart from other Latin American refugees. For the first time, the United States became a country of first asylum for a large group of political refugees fleeing a Communist country in the Western Hemisphere. The United States government assumed long-term financial responsibility in assisting Cubans to resettle, and most important, it practiced an "open-door" policy toward those fleeing Castro's regime. Ironically, those particular characteristics allowed Castro to pursue equally important political objectives. The early flight of Cuba's political and economic elites eliminated a potentially dangerous challenge to Castro's power. Their departure enabled him to consolidate the revolution more swiftly and smoothly, and Castro has periodically used the United States' open-door policy to his own advantage to defuse serious internal political and economic crises.

Exile in the United States was not new for Cuban elites. The United States had often served as a temporary sanctuary for political dissidents during periods of social unrest on the island. Some of Cuba's most noted political leaders, including José Martí, Tomás Estrada Palma, Gerardo Machado, Fulgencio Batista, Carlos Prío Socarrás, and Fidel Castro himself operated from the United States until the political situation in Cuba became more propitious for their return.

The Cuban migration to the United States since 1959 cannot be understood outside its political context, one dominated by the complex triangular relationship between Cuba and the United States, Cuba and the former Soviet Union, and the United States and the Soviet Union. The strong combination of Cold War realities and Cuba's close political and economic relationship with the United States inevitably made the revolution and the migration political, at least from 1959 to 1964. Thus the rules for the migration were dictated mainly by political and not humanitarian considerations. The refugees became a useful, and at times powerful, weapon in the political war between the United States and Cuba.

By January 1961, President Eisenhower, apparently using the Guatemalan coup of 1954 and the Hungarian refugee operation as models, had set the tone for future relations between the United States and Castro's government. Unable to change internal events in Cuba, the United States resolved to overthrow Fidel Castro by force and to embarrass his regime at any opportunity. From 1961 on, the United States opened its doors to all Cubans fleeing "Castro's Communist oppression." The president's measure established an unwritten open-door policy toward refugees from Cuba, a clearly effective action in the short run, since it caused some embarrassment for Castro and drained Cuba of vitally needed professionals. Eisenhower's action fell short of its designed goal, however, as Castro was not overthrown.

The Cuban migration and U.S. efforts to overthrow Castro continued long after Eisenhower left the White House. During Kennedy's administration, commercial flights brought thousands of refugees to Miami, creating a serious problem for the state and federal governments. Kennedy responded to the growing exodus by establishing the Cuban Refugee Center, a program designed to aid

Cuban refugees with financial support and to help them resettle. Moreover, Kennedy accepted Eisenhower's plans to invade Cuba and did so on April 17, 1961. The venture was a military fiasco and a great humiliation for the president.

Despite the Bay of Pigs invasion, direct commercial flights from Havana to Miami continued until October 1962, when U.S. reconnaissance planes discovered Soviet-made offensive missiles in Cuba. The Cuban Missile crisis brought the United States and the Soviet Union to the brink of nuclear war and resulted in the cancellation of all direct flights between Cuba and the United States. As a result, from November 1962 to September 1965, Cubans wishing to come to the United States could do so only through clandestine means, or through restricted flights to third countries like Mexico or Spain.

In 1965 Fidel Castro, facing growing political unrest and widespread economic problems, seized the initiative on refugees by manipulating U.S. immigration policy to his advantage. Knowing that the U.S. open-door policy made it politically awkward, if not impossible, to refuse refugees from Cuba, Castro announced that exiled Cubans could pick up relatives wishing to emigrate at the Port of Camarioca in Matanzas, Cuba. Castro's unilateral "opening" worked; the United States welcomed some 5,000 Cubans to Miami in just a few weeks, and Castro was able to defuse a serious domestic crisis. In November an agreement between Cuba and the United States resulted in the Cuban airlift, which ultimately transported 265,000 refugees to the United States.

The Camarioca boatlift and subsequent airlift took the Johnson administration by surprise, but the president followed his predecessors' policies. He stressed the Cubans' desire for freedom, and provided direct federal aid to Florida and the refugees. Nothing was done to prevent future boatlifts; the United States simply hoped that Castro would not permit them again.

Camarioca, however, was only a prelude. Seven years after the end of the Cuban airlift, Castro launched an even bigger boatlift from the Port of Mariel in Havana. Again there was little the U.S. government could do to stop the frantic, one-way sea traffic from Havana to Key West, Florida. President Jimmy Carter eventually invoked the unwritten open-door policy to admit the 125,000 Cubans who crossed the Florida Straits during the five months the boatlift was in operation. As in the case of Camarioca in 1965, and the Cuban airlift of 1966 to 1973, Castro unilaterally opened and closed the doors to the United States at his convenience.

The Mariel boatlift underlined the contradictions of a blanket open-door policy for refugees from Cuba, especially after it became evident that most Mariel refugees had emigrated for economic, and not political, reasons. Such a discovery created a dilemma for the Carter administration, which had denied refugee status to an estimated 30,000 Haitians on the grounds that they were economic and not political refugees. Carter temporarily solved the dilemma by creating a new immigration classification, "Cuban-Haitian entrant," which provided federal assistance for both groups, but denied them refugee status. The new classification settled the status issue, but it did not solve the problems created by the Mariel influx.

Fifteen years after the Mariel boatlift, most Cubans who went to Peru during the boatlift have been able to obtain entry visas to the United States through the "Exodus" program, sponsored by the Cuban-American National Foundation and authorized by the United States Department of State. However, some 1,500 Mariel "excludables" remain jailed in U.S. federal penitentiaries, some for crimes committed in Cuba, others for crimes committed in the United States; due to their "special" entrant status, they are not entitled to the civil rights all citizens enjoy under the United States Constitution.

Despite the dislocations and problems created by the Mariel boatlift, the United States failed to take the necessary steps to normalize its immigration policy for Cuba and the rest of the hemisphere. Although the Cold War officially ended in 1989, United States immigration and refugee policy for Cuba and Latin America continued to be guided by political considerations. In the case of Cuba, the number of illegal entries increased yearly from 467 in 1990 to 37,139 in 1994.

The politicized nature of United States immigration policy showed its most glaring contradictions during the 1980s. Under the Reagan–Bush and Bush–Quayle administrations, thousands of Haitians continued to brave the perilous 700-mile voyage to Florida, only to be deported back to a politically and economically repressive system. Equally contradictory and inhumane was the deportation of hundreds of thousands of Salvadorans and Guatemalans, most of whom faced certain death at the hands of repressive governments and death squads in their countries. Such is the legacy of a selective open-door policy extended only to refugees fleeing governments unfriendly to the United States.

Opposition to the arbitrary deportation of Haitians and Central Americans grew rapidly during the 1980s, and various civil rights groups engaged in energetic lobbying efforts on the refugees' behalf. The most determined and militant of those groups was the U.S.–based "Sanctuary Movement," an underground network of religious people committed to providing refuge to tens of thousands of Central Americans facing deportation by the Reagan and Bush administrations.

Such strong and well-organized opposition publicly challenged the United States government to come to terms with the fact that the overwhelming majority of refugees trying to gain entrance to the United States were fleeing not Communist repression but U.S.–supported dictatorships. Multiple refugee influxes from Haiti, El Salvador, and Guatemala—all United States allies— brought on a serious crisis in the U.S. Latin American immigration policy. As a result, the federal government faced a difficult decision: whether to open the door equally to all refugees escaping repression, from both the left and the right, or to prosecute thousands of U.S. citizens in the Sanctuary Movement who deliberately broke the law to challenge what they considered to be an unjust foreign policy.

The open-door immigration policy established by Eisenhower— with only Cuban refugees in mind—seemed to have come full circle in the 1980s as more than one million Haitians, Nicaraguans, Salvadorans, and Guatemalans sought political asylum in the United States. Yet, despite the growing number of non-Cuban asylum seekers and the legal paradoxes created by the Mariel boatlift, the United States refused to eliminate the political double standard until 1990.

It is not surprising then, that without a coherent policy to guide him, when President Clinton faced yet another Cuban immigration crisis in 1994, his initial reaction was to rule out negotiations with the Cuban government. Choosing instead to perceive the situation as a short-term crisis—to prove that he could be as anti-Castro as his predecessors—the president again left the door open for more uncontrolled migration from Cuba.

1

The United States, Cuba, and Cuban Exiles, 1868 to 1958

When all the years spent in hope and dispair by Cuban emigres are considered; when the constant and unending sacrifice of exiles is remembered; . . . When one knows that every cent taken from them is one less pleasure for their children, less medicine for the ill, less food on the family table—one cannot but read with profound respect the following words in a letter from Ocala [Florida]: "from this date on we will contribute from our humble wages the insignificant sum of 25 cents a week for the revolution for the independence of our fatherland, Cuba."

José Martí, July 2, 1892

A Legacy of Political Exile

THE MIGRATION OF MORE THAN one million Cubans to the United States since 1959 is not in all respects a unique experience. Since the late 1860s, there have been numerous Cuban migrations, and their causes and patterns were in many ways similar to the post-1959 movement. First, the main reason for the migrations has been overwhelmingly political. Second, Florida, because of its geographic proximity to Cuba and its similar climate, has been home to the largest number of Cubans. Third, most exiles came from the middle and working classes in Cuba. Finally, most Cubans migrated with the original idea of returning home as soon as conditions improved.

Cubans began migrating to the United States and Europe at the oubreak of the war for independence in October 1868. By 1869, it was estimated that over 100,000 Cubans had sought refuge abroad.

A small group of aristocrats who could afford to live in leisurely luxury settled in Europe. A larger group, consisting mainly of middle-class professionals and businessmen, emigrated to New York, Philadelphia, and Boston. A third group, by far the largest, consisted of workers who emigrated to the southeastern United States, most notably to Florida.[1]

The Cuban presence in Florida dates back to the 1830s when Cuban cigar manufacturers, trying to avoid high U.S. tariffs, relocated their operations in Key West. The city provided an ideal setting for cigar production, since it offered easy access to the tobacco regions of western Cuba and the commercial centers of Havana.[2]

Key West became a significant Cuban community in 1869 when Vicente Martínez Ybor, a Spanish cigar manufacturer, moved his operation there from Havana. Soon, skilled cigar workers, escaping the war and Spanish repression in Cuba, were attracted to the city. By 1870 the Cuban population had grown to 1,100, and by 1873 Cubans in Key West constituted a majority of the population.[3]

As the community grew, its members maintained a deep sense of political and human solidarity not only with the pro-independence combatants in Cuba, but also with the newly arrived emigres. In his memoirs, Juan Pérez Rolo, a Key West resident, recalls, "when the steamers arrived from Havana, crowds waited on the docks to welcome the immigrants and to find homes for them."[4]

From its inception, the Cuban community was clearly political both in origin and purpose, and Key West became a center of revolutionary fervor:

> By February 1869, a Cuban colony was thriving in Key West. Revolutionary clubs were organized to raise funds and arm men who were sent to join the expeditionary forces being formed in New York. Key West became a major area of support to the revolutionary effort. According to one Cuban resident, in Key West nothing was discussed except the revolution; each Cuban home was a conspiratorial center; people only thought about the redemption of the fatherland.[5]

José Martí, the political, organizational, and inspirational leader of Cuba's final and decisive offensive against Spain in the 1890s, considered Key West one of the revolution's most important strongholds.[6] He visited there often and mingled with the tobacco workers in their meetings. "The immigrant cigar workers openly contributed 10 percent of their weekly earnings toward the revolution."[7]

Besides the "Cuban cause," Key West exiles became involved in Monroe County politics. By 1875 there were 1,032 registered Cuban voters who were largely responsible for the election of the city's first Cuban mayor, Carlos Manuel de Céspedes, son of the late president of the Cuban republic-in-arms. Céspedes was elected along with a Cuban alderman.[8]

As the Cuban communities in the United States grew and gained political power, their lobbying efforts on behalf of Cuba's liberation began to play a more significant role in Spanish-U.S. relations. The New York junta was an important campaign contributor to candidates amicable to Cuba's liberation. Like Spain, however, the United States believed that its national interests were served by dominating Cuba.

Spain demonstrated its determination to keep Cuba by waging a brutal and expensive thirty-year war against Cuban rebels. The United States had for years shown interest in Cuba. According to historian Lester D. Langley, that interest can be traced back to the earliest days of the American nation:

> Since the founding of the nation, Cuba has occupied a position of preeminence in the Latin American policy of the United States. The writings of Thomas Jefferson, John Adams, James Monroe, Henry Clay, John C. Calhoun, and John Quincy Adams contain numerous references to the strategic and economic importance of Cuba to the United States.[9]

Thus the United States also feared that a truly independent Cuba might have unfavorable consequences for the United States itself. Guided by strong political and strategic interests, the U.S. policy on Cuba, by the 1820s, was clearly defined as one favoring Spanish colonialism over Cuban independence:

> the price of Cuban independence might be British occupation or racial war. Independence for mainland Latin America was both philosophically and politically desirable: The American Revolution served as a prototype of the rejection of Old World rule. Revolution in Cuba, although ideologically desirable, was strategically impractical. In the formation of a Cuban policy, power politics and strategic imperatives outweighed any commitment to an independent Cuba.[10]

Determined to bring Cuba under its control, the United States attempted, on at least four occasions, to buy the island from Spain. In 1869, the U.S. government offered Spain $100 million for Cuba, but Spain, confident that it could quell the revolution, rejected the offer.[11] Another major U.S. offer in 1889 was also rejected.[12]

United States efforts to buy Cuba and bring the island under its control caused a shift in party loyalties among the exiles. At the national level Cubans had customarily voted Republican, but when news of the negotiations spread through the Cuban communities in the United States, Cubans switched their votes and contributions to the Democrats. In the meantime, as the war in Cuba intensified, emigres kept coming to the United States in large numbers, with the resultant establishment of several new communities.

In 1885, Vicente Martínez Ybor, beset by labor problems in Key West, moved his cigar factories to a forty-acre tract of land east of Tampa. Martínez Ybor named the area Ybor City, and its population grew quickly. "Many other manufacturers joined Ybor and within a decade Tampa, including Ybor City, had become the clear Havana tobacco capital. In the process of this transition, thousands of Spanish, Cuban and Italian workers . . . followed the industry to Tampa."[13]

Like their compatriots in Key West, Tampa's Cubans were thoroughly committed to Cuba's independence. Martí, Tomás Estrada Palma, and other members of New York's revolutionary junta came to the city often to raise funds and sometimes to settle labor disputes, since they perceived labor stoppages as a threat to Cuban independence.[14]

According to historian Louis A. Pérez, Jr., in Tampa "class was subordinate to nationalism," and as a result the politics of class became secondary, as both labor and management were on the side of Cuban independence:

> Many leading cigar manufacturers, including Vicente Martínez Ybor and Cecilio Henriquez, publicly identified with Cuban independence. Eduardo Hidalgo Gato, the Key West cigar magnate and close personal friend of Martí, donated tens of thousands of dollars to the separatist cause. Benjamín Guerra, secretary-treasurer of the PRC [Cuban Revolutionary party], owned a cigar factory in Tampa. At the same time, such noted socialist cigarworkers as Carlos Baliño, later one of the founders of the Cuban Communist party, and Diego

Vicente Tejera, organizer of the Cuban Socialist party, labored in exile as close collaborators of José Martí.[15]

While Key West and Tampa have been correctly credited as the vanguard of the Cuban independence efforts abroad, other smaller but equally patriotic Cuban communities never faltered in their support for the cause. Cubans in Ocala, St. Augustine, Jacksonville, West Palm Beach, and Miami contributed tens of thousands of dollars to the New York junta and Martí's Cuban Revolutionary Party.[16]

When Cuba finally gained its independence in 1898, many who had been living in exile in the United States and Europe returned home. For tens of thousands of others, however, the decision was not as easy. Many had been in exile for more than twenty years, and for them Key West, Tampa, or New York City was home. These were the birthplace of their children, where they owned homes and held secure jobs. Going back to Cuba meant starting over in a country ravaged by war, which in some ways was foreign to them and their children. Thus many remained in the United States and contributed much to their communities.

The early Cuban immigrants were responsible for many accomplishments in Key West, Tampa, and Ocala, where they founded the cigar and sugar industries in those cities. Cubans were also responsible for Florida's first labor union and for Key West's first fire department and its first bilingual school.[17] What had started as temporary political exile gradually had turned into a permanent community. Those who came in the nineteenth century left a rich legacy that would continue to serve as an example to their children and grandchildren when they also, for various reasons, chose political exile.

During the first five decades of the twentieth century, smaller groups of Cuban migrants came to the United States to escape political turbulence in Cuba. In the late 1920s and early 1930s, a small group of political and student activists opposed to dictatorial President Gerardo Machado found refuge in Miami and New York City. After Machado's overthrow, most of them returned to Cuba and were replaced in exile by Machado loyalists and the former president himself. The same cycle was repeated, almost without variance, during the presidencies of Fulgencio Batista (1940–1944), Ramón Grau San Martín (1944–1948), Carlos Prío Socarrás (1948–1952), and Fulgencio Batista (1952–1958).[18]

The cycle was not broken in 1959 when a revolutionary government came to power. Batista, following his predecessors' example, was the first to escape the country with his most loyal aides and most of what was left in the national treasury. Six months later, Manuel Urrutia Lleó, the revolutionary government's first president, went into exile.

The revolutionary triumph of 1959 triggered the largest migration ever of Cubans to the United States. In addition to the 600,000 Cubans living in Miami, tens of thousands of Cubans live in most states of the union. Like their predecessors, most of the current emigres came to the United States with the hopes of returning home in a few months or years. Like their predecessors, it is highly unlikely that even in the event of profound political changes in Cuba, many would return home. Time has proven the Cuban exiles' most powerful enemy.

The United States and Cuba, 1898 to 1958

The Cuban war of independence left the island and its people devastated. War-related deaths were estimated at more than 300,000, well over one-tenth of the population, and destruction caused by the war was visible everywhere:

> The number of schools open in 1898 was almost half that open in 1895; before the war there were 90,000 farms and plantations in Cuba; in 1899 only 60,000; 900,000 acres were cultivated in 1899, compared with well over 1,300,000 in 1895. Havana and Matanzas were the worst hit, each cultivating less than one-half what they did before. Only the province of Pinar del Río cultivated more in 1899 than 1895, though many towns of Pinar del Río had been reduced to ashes.[19]

Human and physical destruction were only one aspect of the war damage to the nascent nation. Cuba's principal leaders had been killed during the war, and Cuba was occupied and governed by the U.S. Army for four years. When the government was finally handed to the Cubans on May 20, 1902, the United States left the door open to intervention through the Platt Amendment, which turned Cuba into an American protectorate. The amendment, added by the U.S. Congress to the military appropiations bill of 1900–1901, was subsequently adopted by Cuba's Constituent Assembly by a 16-to-15 vote as part of Cuba's organic law, the

Constitution of 1901. Under the amendment Cuba was forbidden to sign international treaties or lease military bases, except to the United States, and the United States reserved the right to intervene militarily in Cuba for "the preservation of Cuban independence, the maintenance of a government adequate for the protection of life, property, and individual liberty."[20]

Cuba's liberation from Spain, then, did not mean complete independence. From 1902 onward, the United States played such a dominant role in Cuban politics that it was an integral part of the system:

> Under the Platt Amendment, Washington emerged as the center of Cuban politics; increasingly, the Cuban political drama was played for the benefit of an American audience. With foreknowledge of the American commitment to intervene to protect life, property and individual liberty, Cuban leaders organized a political system around the treaty presence of the United States. By the second decade of the Plattist regimen, American policy had become an integral part of Cuban politics and was one of the most active components of the national system.[21]

Washington's political domination was accompanied by monumental increases in U.S. financial involvement. In 1896 U.S. investments in Cuba were estimated at $50 million, mostly in mining and sugar. By 1913 United States investments were estimated to be $220 million—17.7 percent of all U.S. investment in Latin America. United States–owned sugar mill production grew from approximately 15 percent of the Cuban crop in 1906 to 48.4 percent in 1920. By 1928 various estimates placed United States' control of the sugar crop at between 70 percent and 75 percent.[22]

Evidence of U.S. paternalism, and Cuban ruling-class acceptance of it, was clearly underlined in 1906, when President Tomás Estrada Palma, invoking the Platt Amendment, called on Washington to settle a disputed election. The request led to a second U.S. intervention under provisional governor Charles E. Magoon. The intervention, which lasted until 1909, left a mixed legacy. Magoon gave U.S. approval to the traditional practice of pacifying warring political factions by dispensing government sinecures, which became notorious in future Cuban governments. More positively, the provisional governor initiated an extensive public works program that gave Havana a new sewage system. His administration was also responsible for organizing a modern army, for establishing an organic body of law for the executive and the judiciary, and for setting up provincial and municipal governments.[23]

Magoon's interregnum, however, was far-reaching in other, less positive ways. The intervention underlined a number of weaknesses and faults in what Cuban historian Jaime Suchlicki calls the "Platt Amendment Republic," which set the tone for Cuba's problematic political future:

> [The intervention] removed any pretense of Cuban independence, strengthened the Platt Amendment mentality, and increased doubts about the Cubans' ability for self-government. Disillusionment took hold among many leaders, intellectuals, and writers, and this feeling was transmitted to the mass of the population. Cynicism and irresponsibility increased and so did the resort to violence to solve political differences. Even hitherto peaceful racial relations were affected.[24]

United States troops returned to Cuba in 1912 to help President José Miguel Gómez crush a black revolt in Oriente province, which had started over political representation and economic rewards for blacks. Although the Cuban government crushed the revolt by itself, the landing of four marine companies and the presence of the U.S. Navy in Havana reassured the government as it went about killing at least 3,000 rebels.[25]

In the 1920s, U.S. intervention in Cuban politics moved away from armed force and took on more diplomatic, but equally blunt, aspects. In 1920, President Woodrow Wilson, without asking or formally notifying President Mario García Menocal, ordered General Enoch Crowder to Havana to investigate charges of fraud in that year's presidential elections. Crowder was no stranger to Cuban politics. He had served in the Magoon administration, and in 1919, had headed a State Department delegation that rewrote Cuba's electoral law.

Under Crowder's supervision, special elections were held in 1921, and Alfredo Zayas was declared the winner. After the new president took office, Crowder remained aboard his headquarters, the *USS Minnesota*, until late 1922, "dictating to President Zayas on economic, political, and social questions."[26] Earlier in 1922, Crowder had imposed what came to be known as an "honest cabinet," a number of distinguished Cubans, hand-picked by Crowder, to end corruption in government.[27] Crowder's mission was "an intervention in fact if not name."[28]

Legally justified by the Platt Amendment, and guided by political and economic interests, the United States continued interfering in Cuban politics throughout the 1920s. Woodrow Wilson, Warren G. Harding, Calvin Coolidge, and Herbert Hoover had little patience with those who did not fit the State Department's characterization of a desirable Cuban president, who would have a "thorough acquaintance with the desires of this [United States] government" and would be amenable "to suggestion of advice which might be made by the American legation."[29]

When Franklin D. Roosevelt assumed the presidency, a supposedly new era in United States-Latin American relations began. On March 4, 1933, he declared in his first inaugural address, "In the field of world policy, I would dedicate this nation to the policy of the good neighbor—the neighbor who resolutely respects himself and, because he does so, respects the rights of others—the neighbor who respects his obligations and respects the sanctity of his agreements in and with a world of neighbors."[30]

In Cuba, little changed under the Good Neighbor Policy, and Roosevelt's new agenda faced its first critical challenge. A worsening economic situation and increasing political repression under dictator Gerardo Machado led Roosevelt to a partial deviation from nonintervention and to strong diplomacy a la Crowder. As a general strike spread through the island and political opposition to Machado grew stronger, "everyone was asking when the American marines would land."[31]

In April 1933, Secretary of State Cordell Hull sent Sumner Welles to Cuba as ambassador with instructions ostensibly to mediate between Machado and his opposition, but actually to force the dictator out of office with a minimum of turmoil.[32] In August Machado was overthrown, the result of a paralyzing general strike, violent political opposition, and urban terrorism. After gaining the Cuban army's approval, Welles appointed Carlos Manuel de Céspedes to succeed Machado. The son of Cuba's first president during Cuba's war of independence and a prestigious figure, Céspedes soon received U.S. support.[33] Céspedes' government lasted twenty-eight days. He was overthrown by the Directorio Estudiantil Universitario (University Students Directory) and a rebellious army faction led by Fulgencio Batista.

On September 10, 1933, the Directorio, with Batista and the army, appointed Dr. Ramón Grau San Martín as provisional president. The new president had no political experience, but he had won the students' admiration in 1928 when he allowed the expelled Directorio leaders to read their manifesto to his classes at the University of Havana. Grau had also been imprisoned, along with many student leaders, during the anti-Machado struggle.[34] Welles did not approve Grau's presidency and recommended that the United States withhold recognition of his government. Despite Welles' opposition, Grau, urged by the students' strong nationalism and his own perceptions of Cuba's problems, passed a series of progressive decrees that included the eight-hour day, free school lunches, and a minimum wage. United States opposition, however, proved fatal, and Grau was forced to resign by Army Chief Batista on January 14, 1934. From then on, Batista became the new arbiter of Cuban politics. When he appointed Carlos Mendieta as provisional president, the United States quickly recognized the new government. A series of Batista puppets held nominal power between 1934 and 1940.[35]

Grau's government had lasted only one hundred days, but its social reform program left a positive legacy for future generations to consider. Even Batista enacted social reforms. Under his close watch, however, the Presidential Palace became the home of some of Cuba's most notorious thieves. Batista had his own turn as elected president from 1940–1944, became a multimillionaire and ironically was succeeded by Grau, who by then was as corrupt as the others. Carlos Prío Socarrás, another member of the idealistic "generation of 1930" gone bad, followed Grau to the presidency and surpassed his mentor's well-known corruption. In 1952, Batista returned from his self-imposed exile in West Palm Beach, Florida, to lead a bloodless coup and impose a corrupt and repressive dictatorship that lasted until December 31, 1958.

Cuba's brief revolutionary period in 1933 had a far-reaching effect on the politics of the late 1950s. During the latter period, students again played an active role in overthrowing a corrupt and dictatorial government, but what came out of that struggle was radically different from the 1930s. As historian Hugh Thomas noted, the lessons of the 1930s had been well learned: "The revolution of 1959 followed in the wake of that of 1933 as the Second World War followed the First, or the revolution in Russia in 1917 followed that in 1905. The middle class of Cuba received a warning, to which they paid little attention. Afterwards, it was much less easy to expect their radical sons [and daughters] to place faith in liberal solutions."[36]

Notes

1. Louis A. Pérez, Jr., "Cubans in Tampa: From Exiles to Immigrants, 1892–1901," *Florida Historical Quarterly* 57 (October 1978): 129. For a more detailed discussion of the early migrations and exact figures on the different locations, see Fernando Portuondo del Prado, *Historia de Cuba*, 6th ed. (Havana, 1957).

2. Pérez, "Cubans in Tampa," 130. See also Gerardo Castellanos, *Motivos de Cayo Hueso: contribución a la historia de la emigración revolucionaria cubana en los Estados Unidos* (Havana, 1935).

3. Gerald E. Poyo, "Key West and the Cuban Ten-Year War," *Florida Historical Quarterly* 57 (January 1979): 290.

4. Ibid., 291.

5. Gerald E. Poyo, "Cuban Revolutionaries and Monroe County Reconstruction Politics, 1868–1876," *Florida Historical Quarterly* 55 (April 1977): 408–9.

6. José Martí is regarded as the "apostle" of Cuba's independence. As the leader of the Cuban Revolutionary party, he was able to unify all factions fighting against Spain, a move which eventually led to Cuba's liberation after Martí's death in 1895. Besides his active involvement in the revolution, Martí was an accomplished journalist, editor, and philosopher who left twenty-seven volumes of writings, despite the fact that he died at the age of forty-two. See José Martí, *José Martí: Obras Completas*, 27 vols. (Havana, 1975). Of the many Martí biographies published in several languages, Jorge Mañach, *Martí: El Apostol* (Madrid, 1942), remains the best.

7. John C. Appel, "The Unionization of Florida Cigarmakers and the Coming of the War With Spain," *Hispanic American Historical Review* 36 (February 1956): 43.

8. Poyo, "Cuban Revolutionaries," 417.

9. Lester D. Langley, *The Cuban Policy of the United States* (New York, 1968), ix.

10. Ibid., 18–19.

11. Hugh Thomas, *Cuba: The Pursuit of Freedom* (New York, 1971), 250–53.

12. James W. Cortada, "Florida's Relations with Cuba During the Civil War," *Florida Historical Quarterly* 59 (July 1980): 52. For more on U.S. interests in controlling Cuba, see Julio LeRiverend, *Breve historia de Cuba* (Havana, 1978); Emilio Roig de Leuchsenring, *Cuba no debe su independencia a los Estados Unidos* (Havana, 1950); Philip S. Foner, *The Spanish-Cuban-American War and the Birth of American Imperialism*, 2 vols. (New York, 1972); and, by the same author, *A History of Cuba and Its Relations with the United States*, 2 vols. (New York, 1962).

13. Durward Long, "La Resistencia: Tampa's Immigrant Labor Union," *Labor History* 6 (Fall 1965): 194.

14. Pérez, "Cubans in Tampa," 134.

15. Ibid., 134–35.

16. For Martí's own recollections of the Cuban communities in the United States and their fund-raising efforts, see Martí, *Obras Completas*, vol. 10, *En los Estados Unidos* (Havana, 1975).

17. Ileana Oroza, "Hay Raices Cubanas en la Florida," *El Miami Herald*, January 26, 1980, 8.

18. Grau was the only president who did not choose to go into exile after his electoral defeat. Batista, after his overthrow in 1958, went to the Dominican Republic first and to Portugal later. He did not choose the United States because, for political reasons, he was never welcomed by its government, and he felt betrayed by the United States.

19. Thomas, *Cuba*, 423–24. In proportion to Cuba's population of a million and a half before the war, Thomas compares the losses to "Russia's losses in the Second World War, Serbia's in the First World War, and probably double the proportion in the Spanish and American Civil Wars."

20. Russell H. Fitzgibbon, *Cuba and the United States, 1900–1935* (Milwakee, 1935), 272–73. For a comprehensive history of the Platt Amendment see: Emilio Roig de Leuchsenring, *Historia de la enmienda Platt* (Havana, 1935).

21. Louis A. Pérez, Jr., *Intervention, Revolution, and Politics in Cuba, 1913–1921* (Pittsburgh, 1978), xiii. José Martí had always been suspicious of United States intentions in Cuba. Large parts of his copious writings were dedicated to his preocupation with the "monster," as he called the United States. For more on Martí's thoughts on the United States, see Josep Fontana, ed., *José Martí. Nuestra América* (Barcelona, 1970); Philip Foner, ed., *Inside the Monster: Writings on the United States and American Imperialism by José Martí*, translated by Eleanor Randall (New York, 1975); John M. Kirk, "José Martí and the United States: A Further Interpretation," *Journal of Latin American Studies* 9 (November 1977): 275–90.

22. Robert F. Smith, *The United States and Cuba: Business and Diplomacy, 1917–1960* (New Haven, 1960), 17–41.

23. Jaime Suchlicki, *Cuba: From Columbus to Castro* (New York, 1974), 106.

24. Ibid. See also Jorge I. Domínguez, *Cuba: Order and Revolution* (Cambridge, Mass., 1978), 11–53.

25. Domínguez, *Cuba*, 48–49. The revolt's exact death figures are not clear. Some estimates run as high as 7,000, while the government admitted killing 3,000.

26. Ibid., 18.

27. Suchlicki, *Cuba*, 109.

28. Quoted in Thomas, *Cuba*, 548.

29. Quoted in ibid., 549.

30. Edwin Lieuwen, *U.S. Policy in Latin America: A Short History* (New York, 1965), 61.

31. Quoted in Thomas, *Cuba*, 615.

32. Federico G. Gil, *Latin American–United States Relations* (New York, 1971), 160.

33. Suchlicki, *Cuba*, 123.

34. Ibid., 125.

35. Ibid., 129. For more on the post-Machado period, see Luis E. Aguilar, *Cuba 1933: Prologue to Revolution* (New York, 1972); Raúl Roa, *La revolución del 30 se fue a bolina* (Havana, 1979); Jaime Suchlicki, *University Students and Revolution in Cuba, 1920–1968* (Coral Gables, 1969).

36. Thomas, *Cuba*, 605.

2

The Cuban Revolution in the Cold War Context

The bank that underwrites the cutting of the cane is foreign, the consumers' market is foreign, the administrative staff set up in Cuba, the machinery that is installed, the capital that is invested, the very land of Cuba is held by foreign ownership . . . as are, logically enough, the profits that flow out of the country to enrich others.

Fernando Ortiz, 1940

The United States and the Cuban Revolution

FIDEL CASTRO'S TRIUMPHANT MARCH into Havana on January 8, 1959, concluded an insurrection that he and a handful of rebels had initiated only twenty-five months earlier. The overwhelming majority of the Cuban people recognized Castro as a revolutionary hero, who, despite tremendous odds, had defeated the corrupt and brutal dictatorship of Fulgencio Batista.[1] Most important to the majority of Cubans, Castro represented the hope of a new beginning. During the insurrection the rebel leader had promised far-reaching social, economic, and political reforms, and his people anxiously awaited those changes.

In the United States, the initial public reaction to Castro's victory was favorable and hopeful. Most major newspapers provided front-page coverage of the events and high praise for Castro's accomplishments. The *New York Times* editorialized:

> one other thing must be said and this is an acknowledgment to the extraordinary young man, Fidel Castro, who fought against such heavy odds with such tenacity, bravery, and intelligence ever since his pathetically weak band of youths landed in Oriente Province on

December 2, 1956. A great burden now falls on his shoulders, and a task harder in its way than the struggle for liberty that has now ended. The American people will wish him well and all Cubans good fortune.[2]

The editorial was not unusual. The U.S. press had printed many articles about Castro while he was fighting Batista.[3] These articles not only made the American public receptive to the young rebel, but they also helped shape the opinions of several influential leaders. President Eisenhower noted in his memoirs that on more than one occasion, Harry S. Truman had declared: "I think that Fidel Castro is a good young man, who has made mistakes but who seems to want to do the right thing for the Cuban people, and we ought to extend our sympathy and help him to do what is right for them."[4] John F. Kennedy, who would later order the invasion of Cuba, earlier saw Castro as "part of the legacy of Bolivar."[5] Even Eisenhower was seemingly "sympathetic to the aspirations of the new leadership,"[6] at least during the first weeks following the triumph.

The first American actions toward the revolutionary government were cautiously cordial. Within a week the United States recognized the government of Manuel Urrutia Lleó and expressed its desire to work with the new government. The Cuban government's plans were not clear during these early days, however, and any serious attempt to change the status quo would inevitably conflict with U.S. interests in the island.[7]

In 1959, the value of U.S. investments in Cuba was greater than in any other Latin American country except oil-rich Venezuela, and on a per capita basis, the value of U.S. investments in Cuba was more than three times what it was anywhere else in Latin America.[8] By the late 1950s, American capital controlled 90 percent of Cuba's mines, 80 percent of its public utilities, 50 percent of its railways, 40 percent of its sugar production, and 25 percent of its bank deposits. In 1957, American firms made profits of $77 million from their Cuban investments, while employing only a little more than 1 percent of the country's population.[9]

For years Fidel Castro had publicly discussed, analyzed, and proposed remedies for the problems plaguing the Cuban economy.[10] From his headquarters in the Sierra Maestra, Castro had called for land grants to tenant farmers working less than 170 acres, indemnifying owners out of rents over a ten-year period. He also added a provision to guarantee small sugar growers a minimum share of the annual quota at a minimum price. Without mentioning the United States itself, Castro called for the nationalization of the power and telephone companies.[11] Implementation of these reforms would affect U.S. economic interests in Cuba.

The new Cuban leadership also raised important political questions. Whether Castro was a Communist or influenced by communism had long been a key factor in U.S. relations with him. As early as 1957, U.S. government officials had been concerned about what might happen after Batista's inevitable fall from power. They hoped for an orderly transition to a successor government, but Castro was not their choice to lead it.[12] Earl E. T. Smith, the U.S. ambassador, had been searching for a third force to replace Batista for at least a year before Castro's victory. That third force, a "national unity" government, would include the "better elements of the opposition,"[13] but would exclude Castro because "the revolutionaries were attempting to overthrow the government by force."[14]

Smith's preference for a "third force" and his opposition to the revolutionaries underlined a serious contradiction in the United States' Cuba policy. Castro was unacceptable because he was using force to overthrow the government, yet the United States had recognized and fully supported Fulgencio Batista's government, which came to power by forcefully overthrowing the constitutional government of Carlos Prío Socarrás in March 1952.

The United States' main concern in Cuba, however, was less the legality of the government than the ideology of its leaders. Communism, Communist influence, and American economic interests were the real issues. How serious these concerns were would become clear to Castro during his first visit to the United States as the new leader of Cuba.

At the invitation of the American Society of Newspaper Editors, and against the wishes of a "more than irritated" Eisenhower,[15] Castro came to the United States in April 1959. Eisenhower refused to meet with the Cuban leader; as the former president later recalled, the communism question figured prominently in his decision: "Having personally become highly suspicious that Castro was a Communist and deeply disgusted at his murderous persecution of his former opponents, I inquired whether we could not refuse him a visa. Advised that under the circumstances this would be unwise, I nevertheless refused to see him."[16]

During the visit, Castro talked of continued friendship with the United States, defended the trials and executions as just punishment for "war crimes," and offered assurances that all expropriations of foreign-owned property would be legal. He also denied that communism was gaining ground in Cuba.[17] Those public statements differed little from what Castro said in a three-hour conference with Vice-President Richard Nixon. The vice-president, however, in his formal report to the State Department, the White House, and the Central Intelligence Agency, concluded that the Cuban leader was "either incredibly naive about Communism or under Communist discipline," and that "we would have to treat him and deal with him accordingly."[18] Nixon also recommended that the administration organize a force of Cuban exiles to overthrow Castro.[19]

The administration's constant and seemingly obsessive concern with the single question of communism irritated Castro and others in his entourage. "It was as if the United States did not care what Cuba was, provided it was not Communist."[20] Clearly, Castro and the Eisenhower administration differed as to what kind of revolution Cuba should have. Charles C. Alexander summarizes the administration's views:

> Washington wanted Castro to accept United States leadership in the Western Hemisphere, staff his government with people of moderate views, reinstitute civil liberties, and proceed gradually with land reform, compensating American property interests at the prices they asked. In general, the revolution should not overturn the existing foundations of power and influence.[21]

Castro, on the other hand, had repeatedly stated that he would not tolerate manipulation from Washington. Months before his trip to the United States, he had declared that although he wanted good relations with the Eisenhower administration, he would not be submissive to Washington, nor would he sell himself to the United States.[22] Castro probably had in mind what had happened in Guatemala five years earlier.

Eisenhower and the Guatemalan Revolution: A Precedent

By 1959, Washington had extensive experience protecting United States investments in Latin America, as well as preventing communist takeovers and nationalistic reform movements. The United States had a long history of military interventions in the area, and had never been at ease with revolutionary change or even serious reform in its "backyard."[23]

Only five years before Castro's triumph, the Central Intelligence Agency engineered the successful overthrow of the democratically elected, leftist government of Jacobo Arbenz in Guatemala. The Guatemalan president had expropriated unused land belonging to the United Fruit Company, then the country's principal landowner. The American company controlled all of Guatemala's banana exports, ran 580 of the country's 732 miles of railroad, held a monopoly of its telephone and telegraph facilities, possessed its largest electrical plant, and administered one of the most important ports in Guatemala's Caribbean coast.[24] The company also employed numerous publicists in Washington and carried on its board of directors many individuals with ties to the Eisenhower administration.[25] The Guatemalan government's attempts to loosen the hold of the company—resentfully called "the octopus" by Guatemalans—on the national economy set the stage for direct confrontation with Washington.

On June 18, 1954, less than two years after an agrarian reform law had been enacted, a small band of Guatemalan exiles, trained in Honduras and Nicaragua by the Central Intelligence Agency and led by Colonel Carlos Castillo Armas, crossed the border from Honduras into Guatemala. American-piloted CIA planes assisted the invaders by bombing the capital and other cities. Nine days later, President Arbenz resigned, and turned the government over to three loyal military officers. John E. Peurifoy, U.S. ambassador to Guatemala, refused to accept Arbenz's replacements, and began maneuvering for the installation of Carlos Castillo Armas, the CIA's favorite, as president. On July 3, Castillo Armas entered Guatemala City in Peurifoy's embassy plane to take the presidential oath.[26] Upon taking office, the new United States–supported military dictator of Guatemala set out to make the country "safe" for foreign investment again:

The Castillo Armas regime murdered thousands of labor leaders, peasant organizers and political activists, destroyed the labor movement, disfranchised 70% of the voters, including the Indian population, and gave United Fruit not only the uncultivated lands that Arbenz had confiscated, but an additional 800,000 acres under cultivation by independent peasants.[27]

The Guatemalan reformist experience had been ended, and United Fruit's lands had been saved by the CIA.

President Eisenhower did not conceal his happiness with the Guatemalan coup. During a press conference in which he summarized his first two years as president, Eisenhower listed the elimination of the "Communist" threat from Guatemala as one of his proudest accomplishments.[28] The president's happiness turned into patriotic pride when he accepted the credentials of Castillo Armas' newly appointed ambassador to the United States, Lieutenant Colonel José Luis Cruz Salazar:

> The people of Guatemala, in a magnificent effort, have liberated themselves from the shackles of international Communist direction, and reclaimed their right of self-determination. For the people of the United States and for myself, I pay tribute to the historic demonstration of devotion to the cause of freedom given by the people of Guatemala and their leaders. It constitutes living proof of the unity of ideals and aspirations which animate and join us together, and which form the basis of our profound faith in the future.[29]

Eisenhower's attitude toward U.S. intervention in Guatemala made it appear highly unlikely that he would accept a social revolution in Cuba. Nonetheless, Castro too had learned from the Guatemalan experience. His trusted comrade in arms, Ernesto "Ché" Guevara, had personally witnessed the United States' Guatemalan operation, and would wisely advise Castro on how to avoid the costly errors of the Arbenz government.

Cuba, the United States, and the Soviet Union

Many analysts now agree that the United States' concerns over the potential danger posed by the Cuban revolution were so exaggerated and distorted that United States policy makers lost touch with reality. Wayne S. Smith, former Chief of the United States Interest Section in Havana from 1979 to 1982, explains:

By blowing the problem out of proportion, by giving the impression that there was a Cuban under every bush, we unintentionally made Castro look larger than life, omnipresent if not omniscient. In discussing this period [1960s] with a Cuban official, he expressed puzzlement over this very point. He noted: During the 1960s and even up to the present [1980s], the United States has frequently discussed Cuba in such terms as to suggest it is a superpower. The tone is hostile, but you always give us credit for far more capabilities than we have. You flatter us. We often wonder why?[30]

In much the same way, Castro's relationship with the Soviet Union and the latter's supposed designs on Latin America were also highly exaggerated. These views were unfortunate and unjustified in light of many well-known indications to the contrary: (a) Cuba did not have diplomatic relations with the Soviet Union at the time of the revolutionary victory, and would not resume them until May 1960; (b) Castro had never been a member of Cuba's Communist party; (c) the Soviet Union did not have any direct contacts with the revolutionaries until after the victory; (d) the Soviets regarded Latin America as a U.S. sphere of influence, and they did not believe socialist revolutions were possible in the area; and (e) the Cuban Communist Party (PSP) reluctantly endorsed Castro's insurrection only after it had entered its final phase.[31]

Philip W. Bonsal, the United States ambassador to Cuba from 1959 to 1961, agreed with most of those assertions:

Russian skepticism as to how much an asset Castro's erratic personality and leadership could present for Soviet policy in the Western Hemisphere was fully justified. The Russians did not then think of the Cuban Revolution as Marxist-Leninist, though they applauded Castro's hostility toward imperialism. The Soviet Union did not then, in my judgment, contemplate replacing the United States as Cuba's trading partner and economic patron, though Moscow was willing to help Castro harass the United States. I do not believe the Russians wished for a confrontation with the United States over Cuba. I suggest that until July 1960 the Moscow bureaucrats advised Castro to proceed with moderation in his dealings with Washington.[32]

Contrary to popular belief, the Cuban-Soviet relationship grew gradually. In reality, it developed more as a result of events directly affecting Cuba and the United States than Cuba and the Soviet Union. Carla Anne Robbins explains how the widening chasm between the United States and Cuba drove Cuba closer to the Soviet Union:

> Each cabinet shakeup in Havana was greeted in Washington with new alarms that Cuba was going Communist. The thousands of Cuban exiles who streamed into Miami, bearing stories of torture, privation, and Communist infiltration, fanned the flames. The numerous attacks on Cuban shores by exiles stationed in Miami had almost no effect on the Cuban economy or Castro's power, but they did serve to reinforce his suspicions that Washington's failure to stop exile attacks was interpreted as United States hostility. And Cuba's establishment of trade relations with the Soviet Union, Yugoslavia, China, and Poland in the Spring of 1960 was seen in Washington as proof that Cuba was indeed going Communist.[33]

Initially Soviet economic aid to Cuba was limited. The first Cuban-Soviet economic agreement was signed in April 1959 when the Russians agreed to buy 170,000 tons of Cuban sugar, 30,000 tons less than they had bought from Batista in 1958. In February 1960, Anastas Mikoyan, the Soviet deputy premier, led a trade fair to Cuba and offered Havana its first Soviet aid, a 100-million ruble credit to purchase industrial equipment. Yet Cuba and the Soviet Union did not establish diplomatic relations until May 1960, long after relations between Cuba and the United States had begun to deteriorate.[34]

Mikoyan's visit and the resulting Cuban-Soviet trade agreement increased the tension and hostility in U.S.–Cuba relations. In March 1960 President Eisenhower authorized a series of measures designed to overthrow Castro: (a) the termination of sugar purchases, (b) the end of oil deliveries, (c) continuation of the arms embargo in effect since mid-1958, and (d) the organization of a paramilitary force of Cuban exiles to invade the island. Cole Blasier argues that the Cuban government used knowledge of these measures to persuade the Soviet Union to extend aid.[35]

Eisenhower's measures, if uncountered, possibly could have overthrown the revolution. Castro reasoned, not implausibly, that the revolution was in mortal peril. In an effort to protect himself he turned first to the Soviet Union and other socialist countries for means to counter Eisenhower's punitive policies.[36]

Soviet assistance to Cuba began, following the pattern of U.S. actions. Aid denied by the United States was quickly replaced with aid from the Soviet Union. For example, when the United States cut the remaining 700,00 tons of the Cuban sugar quota in July 1960, the Soviet Union added that quantity of sugar to its already existing purchases. Later, when the United States severed diplomatic relations and declared an economic embargo against Cuba, the Soviet Union became Cuba's main trading partner. Robert S. Walters explains how vital Soviet assistance was to Cuba's economy during the early years and subsequent difficult periods:

> Soviet exports to Cuba over the period 1959–63 were dominated by machinery and equipment, fuel, mineral raw materials, metals and food products which in 1963 accounted for almost 75 percent of total Soviet exports to Cuba. It is interesting to note that there was a sharp increase in the export of foodstuffs to Cuba after 1962, when agricultural production, and particularly the sugar crop, fell drastically owing to domestic economic dislocations accompanying Castro's sweeping economic and institutional reforms. This is one of many instances since 1959 in which the domestic economic ills of Cuba were mitigated by exports from the USSR.[37]

Equally vital to the revolution's survival was Soviet and Socialist bloc nations' military aid preceding the Bay of Pigs invasion in 1961. Soviet field artillery and Czech antiaircraft guns poured into Cuba months before the invasion. In addition, the Soviets provided MIG fighters and training for Cuban pilots.[38]

Despite the large economic and military aid Cuba received from the Soviet Union, both nations seemed determined to maintain their ideological distance. Even after Castro proclaimed the "socialist character" of the revolution on April 16, 1961, the Soviet press and Soviet leaders kept referring to the Castro government as a "revolutionary regime" and a "national democracy," not a socialist revolution. The Soviet Union began calling the Cuban revolution socialist only after Castro publicly declared himself a Marxist-Leninist on December 4, 1961.[39]

On his part, Castro repeatedly insisted on Cuba's ideological independence. On several occasions he claimed that every country in the socialist bloc had equal rights, including the right to interpret Marxism-Leninism. Thus he urged the Cuban people to create their own revolutionary institutions according to their conditions, customs, and character. In addition, Castro proudly declared that the Cuban revolution had not been imported from anywhere, that no one had told the Cuban people how to make it, and no one would tell them how to continue making it.[40]

Castro and the Soviet leadership had a number of serious political and ideological clashes after 1961. The most prominent and significant occurred in October 1962, when the Soviet Union negotiated the withdrawal of its missiles from Cuba directly with the United States. Castro was not consulted, and his indignation over the incident led to Cuba's estrangement from the Soviet Union, a closer alliance with the People's Republic of China, and a purge of Cuba's pro-Moscow Communist party (PSP) leaders. Cole Blasier asserts that throughout the 1960s, Castro's personal power was clearly superior to the party's:

> Symbolic of Castro's domestic political supremacy during the 1960s was his summary treatment of the old-guard Communists. When Aníbal Escalante, a leader of the PSP, became too powerful in 1962, Castro dismissed him and sent him abroad. Only one old-guard Communist remained at the top of this organization, and many of the rank and file were purged. Castro turned against the old PSP leadership once more in 1964 (the Marcos Rodríguez affair) and again in 1968. In this latter case, a "microfaction" was charged with conspiring against the Revolution by taking a critical line, a line actually similar to Moscow's. Escalante and others were sentenced to prison for from ten to fifteen years. In this way Castro eliminated some of Moscow's strongest supporters within the old Cuban Communist Party.[41]

The Communist party purges, the post-missile crisis ideological quarrel, and Cuba's closer ties with China were only a few examples indicating that Castro was ideologically independent of Moscow. Economically, however, the Soviet Union has been Cuba's lifeline for more than twenty-five years, and Castro has often expressed Cuba's "eternal gratitude for the generous aid."[42]

Castro's ideological differences with the Soviet Union have never convinced the United States of the feasibility of diplomatic relations with socialist Cuba. Such intransigence is easily understood in light of the two nations' past relations. For more than sixty years, the United States dominated Cuba's political and economic life, and the revolution changed all that almost overnight. As Lester D. Langley put it, "For the first time, a small Caribbean nation, reared in the shadow of American power, successfully challenged American hegemony in the American Mediterranean."[43]

Cuba's historical relationship with the United States, and the fact that its revolution came at the height of the cold war, made the United States government determined to destroy it. United States policy toward the revolution was founded on misconceptions about Castro's ideology and Cuba's relationship with Moscow. Unfortunately, those same misconceptions had been and are the guiding factors for U.S. policy toward most progressive and reformist governments in Latin America, even if they are non-Communist:

> Confusion arises when United States leaders assume that non-Communist leaders are pro-Moscow because they happen to be Leftists or socialists. Such a view overlooks a fundamental distinction, namely that non-Communists are rarely beholden to a foreign power and are dedicated to national causes, whereas the pro-Moscow Communists have strong loyalties and obligations to Moscow.[44]

Moscow had nothing to do with the Cuban revolution's triumph. The revolution took place because socioeconomic and political conditions in Cuba, largely ignored by U.S. investors and policy makers, demanded it. It was after the triumph that the leaders had to face the realities of a bi-polar world, and inevitably choose sides in the cold war.

Notes

1. Scholars have long been interested in the insurrectionary phase of the Cuban revolution and Fidel Castro's rise to power. Thus the period 1952–1959 is represented by an extensive bibliography. See Ramón Bonachea and Marta San Martín, *The Cuban Insurrection, 1952–1959* (New Brunswick, 1974); Rolando E. Bonachea and Nelson P. Valdés, eds., *Cuba in Revolution* (New York, 1972); Robert Taber, *M-26: Biography of a Revolution* (New York, 1961); Carlos Franqui, *Diario de la revolución cubana* (Barcelona, 1976); Robert Freeman Smith, ed., *Background to Revolution: The Development of Modern Cuba* (New York, 1966); Antonio Nuñez Jiménez, *En marcha con Fidel.*, vol. 1, 1959 (Havana, 1982); Mario Mencía, *La prisión fecunda* (Havana, 1980).
2. *New York Times*, January 2, 1959, 24.
3. See Herbert L. Matthews, "An Interview With Fidel Castro," *New York Times*, February 24, 25, 26, 1957; *Time* Magazine, February 25, 1957, 43; January 7, 1957, 33; July 8, 1957, 20, April 14, 1958, 35–36; *Coronet*, February 1948, 77–80; *Look*, February 4, 1958, 19–25; *Nation*, June 29, 1957, 560–63; November 30, 1957, 398–404; *New Republic*, February 27, 1957, 10–14.
4. Dwight D. Eisenhower, *Waging Peace: The White House Years, 1956–1961* (New York, 1965), 524.
5. Ibid.

6. Confidential source quoted in Herbert S. Parmet, *Eisenhower and the American Crusades* (New York, 1972), 561.

7. For first-hand accounts of early U.S. gestures toward the revolutionary government, see Philip W. Bonsal, *Cuba, Castro, and the United States* (Pittsburgh, 1971); Manuel Urrutia Lleó, *Democracia falsa y falso socialismo* (Union City, 1975); and by the same author, *Fidel Castro and Company, Inc.* (New York, 1964).

8. Thomas, *Cuba: The Pursuit of Freedom* (New York, 1971), 1057.

9. Walter LaFeber, *America, Russia, and the Cold War, 1945–1980* (New York, 1980), 212–13; Robert Freeman Smith, *The United States and Cuba: Business and Diplomacy, 1917–1960* (New Haven, 1960), 166–67; Thomas, *Cuba*, 1057–58.

10. During his trial for the attack on the Moncada barracks, Castro, in his own defense, expounded on the main problems of Cuban economic and political life. For the full text of the defense speech, see Fidel Castro, *La historia me absolverá* (Barcelona, 1976).

11. *Nation*, November 30, 1957, 9.

12. Cole Blasier, "The Elimination of United States Influence," in Carmelo Mesa-Lago, ed., *Revolutionary Change in Cuba* (Pittsburgh, 1971), 48; Eisenhower, *Waging Peace*, 521.

13. Earl E. T. Smith, *The Fourth Floor* (New York, 1962), 66.

14. Ibid., 30.

15. Eisenhower, *Waging Peace*, 523.

16. Ibid.

17. *New York Times*, April 25, 1959, 2.

18. Richard Nixon, *Six Crises* (New York, 1962), 352.

19. Theodore Draper, *Castro's Revolution: Myths and Realities* (New York, 1962), 62; Nixon, *Six Crises*, 351–52; Parmet, *Eisenhower*, 561.

20. Thomas, *Cuba*, 1211.

21. Charles C. Alexander, *Holding the Line: The Eisenhower Era, 1952–1961* (Bloomington, Ind., 1975), 259.

22. *Revolución*, January 16, 1959, 8.

23. For more on U.S. military interventions in Central America and the Caribbean, see Jenny Pearce, *Under the Eagle: U.S. Intervention in Central America and the Caribbean* (Boston, 1982); Cole Blasier, *The Hovering Giant: U.S. Responses to Revolutionary Change in Latin America* (Pittsburgh, 1976); Dana Munro, *Intervention and Dollar Diplomacy in the Caribbean, 1900–1921* (New York, 1964); Neale C. Ronning, ed., *Intervention in Latin America* (New York, 1970); Juan José Arévalo, *The Shark and the Sardines* (New York, 1961); Lester D. Langley, *The United States and the Caribbean in the Twentieth Century* (Athens, Ga., 1980); and *The Banana Wars: United States Intervention in the Caribbean, 1898–1934* (Lexington, Ky., 1983).

24. See Stephen Schlesinger and Stephen Kinzer, *Bitter Fruit: The Untold Story of the American Coup in Guatemala* (New York, 1982); Victor Marchetti and John Marks, *The CIA and the Cult of Intelligence* (New York, 1975); David Wise and Thomas Ross, *The Invisible Government* (New York, 1964); Harry Rositzke, *The CIA's Secret Operations* (New York, 1977); North American Congress on Latin America (NACLA), *Guatemala* (New York, 1974); Richard H. Immerman, *The CIA in Guatemala* (Austin, 1982); and George Black, Milton Jamil, and Norma Chinchilla, *Garrison Guatemala* (New York, 1984).

25. Stephen Schlesinger, "How Dulles Worked the Coup d' Etat," *Nation*, October 28, 1978, 440. See also Thomas McCann, *An American Company: The Tragedy of United Fruit* (New York, 1976); NACLA, *Guatemala*.

26. NACLA, *Guatemala*, 51.

27. Mary Jezer, *The Dark Ages: Life in the United States, 1945–1960* (Boston, 1982), 73; Langley, *The United States in the Caribbean*, 210.

28. Immerman, *The CIA in Guatemala*, 5.

29. Ibid.

30. Carla Anne Robbins, *The Cuban Threat* (New York, 1983), xii-xiii.

31. These points are supported by a rich literature on Soviet-Cuban relations, including Cole Blasier, *The Giant's Rival: The USSR and Latin America* (Pittsburgh, 1983); Blanca Torres Ramírez, *Las relaciones cubano-sovieticas, 1959–1966* (Mexico, 1971); Andrés Súarez, *Cuba: Castroism and Communism, 1959–1966* (Cambridge, 1967); Angel García and Piotr Mironchuk, *Esbozo histórico de las relaciones entre Cuba-Rusia, Cuba-URSS* (Havana, 1976); Carla Anne Robbins, *The Cuban Threat* (New York, 1983); Lynn Darrell Bender, *The Politics of Hostility: Castro's Revolution and United States Policy* (Hato Rey, P.R., 1975); F. Parkinson, *Latin America, the Cold War and the World Powers, 1945–1973* (Beverly Hills, 1974); Lester D. Langley, *The Cuban Policy of the United States: A Brief History* (New York, 1968).

32. Bonsal, *Cuba, Castro and the United States*, 154–55.

33. Robbins, *The Cuban Threat*, 17. For some popular mass-market works on the "Soviet conspiracy" to take over Cuba, see Jay Mallin, *Fortress Cuba: Russia's American Base* (Chicago, 1965); Daniel James, *Cuba: The First Soviet Satellite in the Americas* (New York, 1961); Warren Miller, *90 Miles From Home: The Truth from Inside Castro's Cuba* (Greenwich, Conn., 1961); Mario Lázo, *Dagger in the Heart: American Foreign Policy Failures in Cuba* (New York, 1968); Leovigildo Ruíz, *Diario de una traición: Cuba 1959* (Miami, 1965); Theodore Draper, *Castro's Revolution: Myths and Realities* (New York, 1962); and *Castroism: Theory and Practice* (New York, 1965).

34. Robbins, *The Cuban Threat*, 17.

35. Blasier, *The Giant's Rival*, 103.

36. Blasier, *The Hovering Giant*, 195.

37. Robert S. Walters, "Soviet Economic Aid to Cuba," in James Nelson Goodsell, ed., *Fidel Castro's Personal Revolution in Cuba: 1959–1973* (New York, 1975), 170.

38. Peter Wyden, *Bay of Pigs: The Untold Story* (New York, 1979), 103.

39. Torres Ramírez, *Las Relaciones cubano-sovieticas*, 44–45.

40. Ibid., 74.

41. Blasier, *The Giant's Rival*, 104–5. For details on the purges, see Súarez, *Cuba: Castroism and Communism*; K. S. Karol, *Guerrillas in Power: The Course of the Cuban Revolution* (New York, 1970); Irving Horowitz, ed., *Cuban Communism* (New Brunswick, 1977).

42. Fidel Castro, "Nos enfrentaremos al porvenir con la experiencia de veinte años y el entusiasmo del primer día" (Havana, 1979), 27. For more on Castro's views of Cuba-USSR relations, see Michael Taber, ed., *Our Power Is That of the Working People: Building Socialism in Cuba, Fidel Castro Speeches*, vol. 2 (New York, 1983).

43. Langley, *The U.S. in the Caribbean*, 211.

44. Blasier, *The Giant's Rival*, 155.

3

Eisenhower and the Cuban Migration: The Door Is Opened

Our people opened their homes and hearts to the Hungarian refugees four years ago. I am sure we will do no less for the distressed Cubans.

Dwight D. Eisenhower, January 18, 1961

Setting the Tone

THE POLITICAL AND ECONOMIC PROGRAMS of the Castro government soon came into conflict with those most adversely affected by the new order: the political and economic elites, both foreign and native. The former could make appeals through their governments to protect their interests, which in the case of the United States eventually led to the break in diplomatic relations with Cuba. For the native elites, however, the options were few, they could oppose the government, at extremely high risk, or leave the country.

As Castro steadily consolidated his power, the option for the Cuban elites was limited to emigration. This decision was not ultimately in the hands of the disaffected Cubans. Their future depended on the willingness of the United States to accept them.[1]

Cuban exiles had posed a problem for the Eisenhower administration from the first day of the revolution, when some 500 followers of deposed dictator Fulgencio Batista entered the United States and were granted political asylum.[2] This first "crack in the door" led to more than 7,000 political exiles in 1959 alone. This number increased almost tenfold in less than a year (see Table 3.1).[3]

Table 3.1 Cuban Refugees in Florida, 1950–1959

Year	Immigrated	Naturalized
1950	2,179	718
1951	1,893	775
1952	2,536	817
1953	3,509	982
1954	5,527	1,482
1955	9,294	1,921
1956	14,953	1,372
1957	13,733	1,344
1958	11,581	1,323
1959	7,021	1,319
Total	72,226	12,053

Source: Cabinet Paper, *Cuban Refugees in Florida* (Abilene, Kan.: Dwight D. Eisenhower Library, November 8, 1960); Series W. H. O. Cabinet Secretariat, Folder CI-72.

President Eisenhower's decision to allow immigration from Cuba was not hastily made. It was carefully studied and motivated by several factors: (a) humanitarian concerns, (b) the desire to overthrow the revolution with exile forces, (c) the wish to embarrass the Cuban government, and (d) the knowledge that many of the exiles could easily be assimilated because they had been linked by profession, business, education, and culture to the United States.[4]

In the short run, the administration's decision was a sound one. The United States had much to gain and little to lose by welcoming disaffected Cubans. If nothing else, the propaganda effect of a massive exodus from a Communist country to a capitalist one was tremendous. United States Representative Walter H. Judd (Republican of Minnesota) was quick to interpret the migration in ideological terms: "Every refugee who comes out [of Cuba] is a vote for our society and a vote against their society."[5]

Although the United States achieved an important propaganda victory, the most important impact of the early exodus was its impact on the Cuban economy.[6] The first refugee wave was largely of middle- and upper-class people with professional training or skill. According to Castro, Cuba lost more than 50 percent of its doctors and teachers to the United States during the first two years of revolution.[7]

While the refugee flow continued unabated through 1959, relations between the United States and Cuba deteriorated rapidly. In June 1960, American oil refineries in Cuba refused to process Russian crude oil. Later that month, four American-owned hotels and the refineries were nationalized. On July 5, the Cuban cabinet authorized the nationalization of all U.S. property in Cuba. In retaliation, President Eisenhower canceled Cuba's sugar quota, declaring: "This action amounts to economic sanctions against Cuba. Now we must look ahead to other moves: economic, diplomatic, and strategic."[8]

The official break of diplomatic relations between the United States and Cuba came on January 3, 1961.[9] Before the break, however, President Eisenhower had established the public tone and guidelines for implementing the United States immigration policy towards Cuba. On March 17, 1960, the president made a dramatic plea to Congress to accept more immigrants for "humanitarian reasons."[10] Eisenhower's "humanitarian" plea was a thin veneer for the secret actions he had taken just a few hours before speaking to Congress in ordering the CIA to organize, arm, and train Cuban exiles for a possible invasion of Cuba.[11]

After the diplomatic break, Eisenhower's rhetoric in reference to the migration from Cuba acquired a belligerent tone typical of that cold war period. The humanitarian image of a "better life" of less than a year earlier suddenly changed to escape from the terror of "Communist oppression."[12] From 1961 on, the U.S. government claimed that the American people had opened their "homes and hearts" to the "distressed Cubans fleeing from Communist oppression."[13]

The diplomatic break also meant that those who wished to emigrate to the United States would have to do so through a third-country route, traveling first to Spain, for example, where they could apply for U.S. entry visas. Fortunately for Cubans wishing to go to the United States, the situation was soon changed when the United States Department of State and Department of Justice began the visa-waiver procedure, allowing the visa requirement to be set aside in "emergency" cases.[14]

The visa-waiver procedure allowed continued direct migration from Cuba to the United States, even though the two countries no longer had diplomatic relations. From January 3, 1961, any Cuban who claimed to be "fleeing from Communist oppression" qualified for a visa-waiver to enter the United States. Eisenhower left the White House later that month, but by that time his actions had set the tone for U.S. immigration policy toward Cuba and for U.S.–Cuba relations until the present.

The Hungarian Refugees: A Precedent

When President Eisenhower called on the American people to "open their homes and hearts" to Cubans he regarded as fleeing Fidel Castro's Communist oppression, he did not ask for anything new. Almost four years earlier, during his State of the Union message of January 10, 1957, the president used similar words in reference to Hungarian refugees: "The recent historic events in Hungary demand that all free nations share to the extent of their capacities in the responsibility of granting asylum to victims of Communist persecution."[15]

The Soviet Union's invasion of Hungary in October 1956 took most U.S. policy makers by surprise. With no sound understanding of the revolt nor of the Soviet response to it, the administration reacted by establishing an emergency program to help thousands of Hungarian refugees pouring into Vienna.[16] The administration's reaction escalated the Hungarian crisis into a serious cold war confrontation, and placed the refugees at the center of it.[17]

President Eisenhower committed his administration to "rescuing" at least 21,500 refugees, transporting them to the United States, and helping them resettle as soon as possible. The president appointed Tracy S. Voorhees to head the President's Committee for Hungarian Refugee Relief, which would coordinate all relief efforts by voluntary and government agencies.[18] While the President's Committee arranged the details of resettlement, the transatlantic air and sea lift of refugees proceeded smoothly. Once in the United States, the refugees were taken to Joyce Kilmer Reception Center at Camp Kilmer, New Jersey, where they got their first taste of American life.[19]

The refugees' arrival in the United States did not escape the cold war furor of the period. Nearly every aspect of the Hungarian relief operation was somehow framed in anti-Soviet and pro-United States rhetoric. The *New York Times* reported the arrivals with such headlines as "First Group of Refugees From Communist

Oppression in Hungary Arrives in New Jersey on Way to New Homes."[20] Wilber M. Bruckner, head of the welcome delegation at Kilmer Reception Center, greeted the first refugees with a lecture on the differences between life in the Soviet Union and the United States, and with a patriotic exhortation: "Compare the way the Soviet Union treats its colonies and the freedom in this country which you will see. . . . I want to initiate you, I want you to know what freedom is all about. First I want you to applaud the flag . . . now make it your first act on American soil to applaud the American flag."[21]

Anti-Communist rhetoric was far from spontaneous, since the White House made sure that the media always had enough "horror stories" of life under communism. For that purpose, Gaspar Hargitai's letter to the president was made public in a White House press package:

> We the Hungarian refugees, who have experienced under Communism constant persecution, deprivation and perpetual fear of the violation of our personal liberties, are particularly able to appreciate that magnificent, humane treatment which the total Western Nations . . . have accorded us.
>
> Mr. President: many of those compelled to stay in Hungary have requested me to report the unendurable conditions that have been created in Hungary under Communism and that have resulted in the total liquidation of certain groups in our society.[22]

Tracy S. Voorhees also chose strong anti-Communist language to explain the meaning of the refugee relief operation. In his final report to the president, the chairman of the Committee for Hungarian Refugee Relief stated: "While Russian tanks were firing on Hungarians, United States military planes and ships were carrying many thousands of them to the safe haven of our free land. Like the Berlin airlift, the meaning of this operation was not lost on the peoples of the world."[23] Mr. Voorhees was right. The plight of the Hungarian refugees attracted world attention, and the U.S. role in their rescue was justly lauded. What Voorhees failed to mention in his report was the fact that the administration's "humanitarian" rescue mission was limited to those who passed the rigorous screening process in Vienna.

In a memorandum explaining U.S. policy for assisting refugees from Hungary, Luther Reid stated that excepting hardship cases, only those best fitted for integration into the American economy would be granted asylum in the United States:

> Those to be brought to the United States both from Austria and countries of second asylum will be refugees selected on the basis of hardship cases such as those involving broken families, and special interest cases such as scientists, engineers, etc., whose skills will enable them to be integrated readily into the American economy.[24]

The selection process worked almost perfectly. According to statistics compiled at the Joyce Kilmer Reception Center, as of February 13, 1957, 23,474 of 24,510 Hungarian refugees had been resettled. Such success can be attributed to the refugees' high educational level. The average length of education among the refugees was almost ten years; nearly a thousand had four years of college or more (see Table 3.2).[25] It is not surprising that within months after their arrival the Hungarian refugees were hailed by some as "the most successful mass migration in American history."[26]

Whether the Hungarians' was the most successful mass migration or not is highly debatable. First, it was not massive, since only 38,000 made the trip. Second, there is no reliable data to measure the Hungarians' success against other immigrant groups such as the Italians or Germans. Nonetheless, for the Eisenhower administration, the Hungarian refugee operation was clearly a success. Nearly everything worked according to plan. The screening was quick and accurate, the transportation smooth and without incident, resettlement swift, and the propaganda hit scored against the Soviets invaluable.

The Hungarian refugee operation's overwhelming success convinced the administration that it could solve another refugee crisis from a Communist country the same way. Thus, when Cuban refugees began flowing into Miami, President Eisenhower did not hesitate to use the same rhetoric, the same format, and to again appoint Tracy S. Voorhees to head a Presidential Commission on Cuban Refugees. The Cuban migration however, did not fit the Hungarian blueprint, and it would be up to Eisenhower's successors to come up with their own ways of coping with the seemingly incessant Cuban migration.

Table 3.2   Basic Statistics on Hungarian Refugees at Kilmer Reception Center (December 25, 1956, to January 17, 1957)

	Number	Average Age
Males	4,260	28 yrs., 8 mos.
Females	1,461	30 yrs., 3 mos.
Total number speaking English		705
Total having relatives in U.S.A.		2,505
Average family size		3 (1 child)
Educational attainment		
Less than 4 years		8
Elementary 4-year course		2,106
Technical 4-year course		1,666
Gymnasium 8-year course		1,175
University 4-year course		607
Professional Engineering degree		71
Master's degree		19
Doctorate degree		69
Average length of education		9 yrs., 10 mos.

Occupational Categories	Number	Percent
Students	278	4.8
Professional and managerial	1,011	17.6
Clerical and sales	616	10.8
Services	343	6.0
Agricultural, fishery, forestry, etc.	185	3.3
Skilled	1,751	30.6
Semi-skilled	972	17.0
Unskilled	564	9.9
Total	5,721	100.0

Note: Figures are based on a sampling of 5,721 employable refugees 16 years of age and older, excluding housewives and persons physically unable to work.

Source: Memorandum, Tracy S. Voorhees to Trustees of the Institute of International Education, Inc., February 14, 1957. Eisenhower Papers, Eisenhower Library.

The Cuban Children's Program

The most bizarre episode of the Cuban migration to the United States during the Eisenhower administration was the Cuban Children's Program, a scheme to rescue Cuban children supposedly escaping Communist indoctrination. The program began in 1960 as a result of wild rumors circulating in Cuba and the exile community in Miami about Castro's revolutionary programs. One of the most sensational and powerful of those rumors was the one about the "patria potestad," or the rights of parents over their children.

According to copies of a purported new Cuban decree that circulated through the underground network in Cuba:

> All children will remain with their parents until they are three years old, after which they must be entrusted to the Organización de Círculos Infantiles [state day-care centers]. Children from three to ten would live in government dormitories and would be permitted to visit their parents no less than two days a month. . . . Older children would be assigned to the most appropiate place and thus might never come home.[27]

Other stories related that children were picked up off the streets and never seen again; that orphanages, such as Casa Beneficiencia, had been emptied and all children sent to the Soviet Union for indoctrination, and that in the town of Bayamo, fifty mothers had signed a pact to kill their children rather than hand them to Castro.[28]

Despite Castro's public declarations that the "patria potestad" document was "a forgery put out by the Cuban underground and the United States Central Intelligence Agency to discredit his regime,"[29] the rumors continued. In the meantime, secret talks began between Monsignor Bryan O. Walsh and State Department officials, in an attempt to "save the children."[30] Out of those discussions came operation "Pedro Pan," designed to "help Cuban parents send their children unaccompanied to the United States to avoid Communist indoctrination."[31] The operation later evolved into the Cuban Children's Program, intended to provide foster care for Cuban refugee children sent unaccompanied to the United States by their parents. According to Walsh, the operation was granted "blanket authority to issue visa-waivers to all children between the ages of six and sixteen."[32]

The Eisenhower administration's decision to undertake the Cuban Children's Program (see Table 3.3) broke with traditional U.S. immigration policy. Never before had the United States government-funded foster care of refugee children in the United States. Previous child refugee programs had been supported by private organizations, church groups, and individual donations.[33]

News of a U.S. government-funded foster service for children escaping "Communist indoctrination" spread throughout Cuba like wildfire. Soon there were thousands trying to get their children out, some for no apparent reason.[34] On December 26, 1960, the first unaccompanied children—ten teenage boys—arrived in Miami. By the summer of 1961, about 200 children reached Miami each week.

Alarmed by the large number of unaccompanied children arriving in Miami, and concerned about the causes for the unexpected migration, the U.S. Senate held hearings on the Cuban Children's Program. Unfortunately, the hearings produced little more than a number of emotional and unsubstantiated allegations about the

Table 3.3   The Cuban Children's Program

Agency	Number served	Percent of total
Catholic Welfare Bureau	7,041	84.5
Children's Service Bureau	365	4.4
Jewish Family and Children's Service	117	1.4
United HIAS Service	28	0.3
Florida State Department of Public Welfare	780	9.4
Total	8,331	100.0

		Cost
Amount paid for foster care		$27,108,131.75
In foster family homes	$ 9,248,479.68	
In institutions or group homes	$17,859,652.07	
Amount paid for special services and transportation of children		$ 1,423,357.33
Total expenditures		$28,531,489.08

Source: U.S. Department of Health, Education and Welfare; Social and Rehabilitative Services, Children's Bureau; "Cuba's Children in Exile" (1967), 6.

Cuban indoctrination program. For example, Wendell N. Rollerson, director of the Inter-American Affairs Commission, which was organized in 1959 to assist the Miami community with the Cuban refugee influx, testified that some children were being sent to the Soviet Union for Communist indoctrination. He provided little or no evidence to support the charges in his testimony. Rollerson said only that he knew 1,600 Cuban children had been taken to the Soviet Union in one shipload, and that some parents had received letters of disaffection from them. The allegation was never verified.[35]

The United States mass media rose to the occasion and dramatically pointed out the urgency of the matter. The *U.S. News & World Report*'s treatment of the children's exodus provides a good example of the political tone given to the sensitive human tragedy: "Why do Cubans send their children into exile? The big reason is to get them away from the Communist brainwashing that is universal in Cuban schools. It starts with the alphabet, and it extends through every school activity."[36]

In the same fashion, the *New York Times* emphasized the parents' determination to prevent their children's indoctrination:

> These parents would rather entrust their children to relatives, friends or strangers in the United States than permit them to be indoctrinated with Communist ideas. Castro's Cuba Communist indoctrination starts in the kindergarten and has to a great degree been substituted for education in all schools of the island.[37]

Little was said, however, about the dramatic, and in most cases traumatic, situation the children faced: separation from their parents, arrival in a strange land, a language barrier, and adaptation to a new culture and environment. These emotional transformations went largely unnoticed by the media, as the children were quickly scattered in more than a hundred communities from Miami, Florida, to Yakima, Washington.[38]

Most children who participated in the Cuban children's program were told by their parents that their separation would last only a few weeks or months. But events in Cuba (the Bay of Pigs fiasco in April 1961 and the missile crisis of October 1962) extended the separation for longer than anyone anticipated. Many of the 14,048 children who came to the United States during the program waited up to twenty years for family reunification.

Notes

1. Domínguez, *Cuba: Order and Revolution* (Cambridge, Mass., 1978), 140.
2. *New York Times*, January 3, 1959, 3; *Miami Herald*, January 2, 1959, 2.
3. Cabinet Paper, "Cuban Refugees in Florida," 8 November 1960, Eisenhower Papers, Series "Cabinet Secretariat," Eisenhower Library, Abilene, Kansas.
4. Domínguez, *Cuba*, 140.
5. *New York Times*, May 23, 1959, 1. In a letter to President Eisenhower, Ira F. Willard, chairman of the Cuban Refugee Committee, refers to Dade County, Florida, as a "front line in the Cold War." Ira F. Willard to Dwight D. Eisenhower, 17 October 1960, Eisenhower Papers, File "Cuban Refugees 1960–61," Eisenhower Library.
6. Richard R. Fagen, Richard A. Brody, and Thomas O'Leary, *Cubans in Exile: Disaffection and Revolution* (Stanford, 1968), 16.
7. Fidel Castro, *Informe Central al Primer Congreso del Partido Comunista de Cuba* (Havana, 1976), 116–23, 133–38.
8. Paul Hoeffel and Sandra Levinson, eds., "The U.S. Blockade: A Documentary History," *Cuba in Focus*, December 1979, 6.
9. Like the insurrectionary period of the revolution, the history of U.S. relations with Cuba and the events leading to the break in diplomatic relations have been the theme of several important works. See Lester D. Langley, *The Cuban Policy of the United States: A Brief History* (New York, 1968) and *The U.S., Cuba, and the Cold War: American Failure or Communist Conspiracy* (Lexington, Ky., 1970); Robert D. Crassweller, *Cuba and the U.S.: The Tangled Relationship* (New York, 1971); Philip W. Bonsal, *Cuba, Castro, and the United States* (Pittsburg, 1971); Darrell Lynn Bender, *The Politics of Hostility: Castro's Revolution and United States Policy* (Hato Rey, Puerto Rico, 1975).
10. *State Department Bulletin*, March 25, 1969, 659.
11. Peter Lyon, *Eisenhower: Portrait of the Hero* (Boston, 1974), 807.
12. Dwight D. Eisenhower, *Public Papers of the Presidents of the United States, 1960–1961* (Washington, D.C., 1953–1961), 1059.
13. Eisenhower, *Public Papers*, 1059.
14. *State Department Bulletin*, January 17, 1961, 659–60.
15. Lawton Collins to Mrs. D. May, 1 February 1957, Eisenhower Papers, File "Questions, Comments, Suggestions," Eisenhower Library.
16. Douglas J. Hedli, "United States Involvement or Non-Involvement in the Hungarian Revolution of 1956," *International Review of History and Political Science* 11 (1974): 72–78.
17. For more on the Hungarian revolt and its implications for the cold war between the United States and the Soviet Union, see Janos Radvaniji, *Hungary and the Superpowers: The 1956 Revolution and Realpolitick* (Stanford, 1972); Oscar Jaszi, *Revolution and Counter-Revolution in Hungary* (New York, 1969); Richard Lettis and William E. Morris, eds., *The Hungarian Revolt: October 23–November 4, 1956* (New York, 1961); Bela K. Kiraly and Paul Jonas, eds., *The Hungarian Revolution of 1956 in Retrospect* (New York, 1978).
18. "Committee for Hungarian Relief Submits Final Report," *Department of State Bulletin*, June 17, 1957, 984.
19. "They Begin Again: The Story of the Refugees at Kilmer," Files of the President's Committee for Hungarian Refugee Relief. Box 19, Immigration Information, Eisenhower Library. This sixteen-page booklet prepared by the Presi-

dent's Committee showed the pleasant life the refugees enjoyed at Kilmer and the wide selection of consumer goods available to them there.

20. *New York Times*, November 22, 1956, 1.

21. Ibid.

22. Gaspar Hargitai to Dwight D. Eisenhower, 15 January 1957, Eisenhower Papers, Series "Hungarian Refugee Relief," Eisenhower Library.

23. "Report by President's Committee for Hungarian Relief," *Department of State Bulletin*, June 17, 1957, 984.

24. Memorandum, Luther Reid to Max Rabb, "Hungary," Eisenhower Papers, Eisenhower Library.

25. Memorandum, Tracy S. Voorhees to Trustees of the Institute of International Education, Inc., February 14, 1957, Eisenhower Papers, Eisenhower Library.

26. *New York Times*, March 24, 1957, 1; *Wall Street Journal*, January 31, 1957, 1.

27. *Time* Magazine, October 6, 1961, 41.

28. The rumor's origins are still unknown, but for a good firsthand account of some of the false stories and their effects on the children and their parents, see Grupo Areíto, *Contra viento y marea* (Havana, 1978), 32–48.

29. Castro's assertions were as good but no better than anyone's. There is still no concrete evidence to confirm the rumor's origins. For Castro's speech see *Bohemia*, May 27, 1960, 67–69.

30. It must be noted that the program originated as an attempt to "save" those children who had attended the elite Reston Academy, an American school in Havana. See Monsignor Bryan O. Walsh, "Cuban Refugee Children," *Journal of Interamerican Studies and World Affairs* 3–4 (July–October 1971): 389.

31. Ibid., 396.

32. Ibid., 402.

33. Ibid.

34. María Masud, the author's wife, and her brother, Roberto González, came to the United States unaccompanied as part of the Cuban Children's Program. She declares that her parents, like many others she knew, "just went with the rumor and got their children out before they [the children] could be sent to Russia for Communist indoctrination." Interview with María Masud, Tallahassee, Florida, November 22, 1984. The author, although not part of the Children's Program, also came to the United States (October 15, 1961) as a result of the "patria potestad" rumor. Interview with Victoria Piloto and Félix Masud, Sr., Miami, Florida, December 20, 1982. For more firsthand accounts of the Children's Program and life in the foster camps, see Grupo Areíto, *Contra viento y marea*; Jesus Díaz, *De la patria y el exilio* (Havana, 1979); Alex López, "Dos años en Matacumbe y Florida City: entrevista con Alex López," *Areíto* 5 (1978): 13–19.

35. *New York Times*, December 8, 1961, 24.

36. *U.S. News & World Report*, March 19, 1962, 16. It is imperative to note that the "brainwashing" illustrations the article alluded to were from a primer that portrayed Castro and his brother Raúl as patriots in much the same way an American primer would describe George Washington or Thomas Jefferson.

37. *New York Times*, March 9, 1963, 1.

38. Kathryn Close, "Cuban Children Away from Home," *Children* 10 (January 1963): 3.

4

Kennedy and the Cuban Migration

This country has always served as a lantern in the dark for those who love freedom but are persecuted, in misery, or in need.

John F. Kennedy, July 1961

Kennedy and Castro

ON NOVEMBER 9, 1960, John Fitzgerald Kennedy became the youngest president-elect in United States history. His youth, vitality, intelligence, and charisma gave his administration—the New Frontier—a dynamism unlike any other in the twentieth century. Kennedy's election was hailed as the beginning of a new era. Eight years of conservative republicanism would be replaced by a new generation unafraid of change and risk. In his inaugural address, the new president expressed his administration's approach:

> Let the word go forth from this time and place, to friend and foe alike, that the torch has been passed to a new generation of Americans—born in this century, tempered by war, disciplined by a hard and bitter peace, proud of its ancient heritage—and unwilling to witness or permit the slow undoing of those human rights to which this nation has always been committed, and to which we are committed today at home and around the world. . . . Let us never negotiate out of fear, but let us never fear to negotiate.[1]

Kennedy did not mention Castro or Cuba in the address, so it was not clear whether his administration would be willing to negotiate with the Cuban government. Candidate Kennedy's rhetoric, however, indicated a determination to pursue a hard-line Cuba policy. During a campaign speech he referred to Castro as a real threat to the United States: "Castro has transformed the island into a hostile and militant Communist satellite, a base from which to carry Communist subversion throughout the Americas." On October 15, 1960 he declared: "We must let Mr. Castro know that we do not intend to be pushed out of our naval base in Guantanamo." And in true cold war tone, he sent the Soviet Union a stern warning: "We must let Mr. Khruschev know that we are permitting no expansion of his foothold in our Hemisphere—and that the Organization of American States will be given real strength and stature to resist any further Communist penetration by whatever means necessary."[2] The candidate's tone was understandable, since plans and preparations for the invasion of Cuba were well advanced at the height of the campaign. In addition, the young Democrat had to prove that he was as anti-Communist as his opponent, Vice-President Richard M. Nixon.

The anti-communism issue had dominated U.S. politics since February 9, 1950, when Joseph R. McCarthy, a U.S. senator from Wisconsin, accused the State Department of being full of Communists. The senator's pronouncement developed into an anti-Communist phobia that affected politicians, public servants, and professionals at almost every level of government, industry, academia, and show business. Thousands of "suspected" Communists were purged from their jobs, and politicians not considered strong anti-Communists had little or no chance of winning elections.

Democrats were especially vulnerable to McCarthyism's wrath. For years the party had been blamed for being "soft" on communism, "losing" China, Soviet expansion in Eastern Europe, and Communist "infiltration" in the U.S. government. Viewed in this context, Kennedy's words were not surprising.[3]

Castro, who hoped a new administration would bring better relations with the United States, and who knew about Eisenhower's invasion plans, reacted to Kennedy's remarks by calling him an "ignorant, illiterate, beardless kid."[4] Thus when Kennedy took office in January 1961, U.S.–Cuban relations continued their accelerated pace toward open confrontation.

Less than three months later, and working under the assumption that a massive revolt against Castro would break out as soon as exile forces landed on Cuban beaches, President Kennedy authorized the invasion of Cuba as planned by the Eisenhower administration. The timing of the invasion—April 17, 1961—was nearly perfect, since Cuba's economy was experiencing its most difficult post-revolution period. The diplomatic break with the United States, the nationalization of key industries, and the emigration of thousands of technicians were beginning to take their toll:

> In the space of a few months Cuba had transformed the structure of ownership and management in all sectors of the economy. Simultaneously it had totally changed both its sources of supply and its export market. Moreover, these upheavals coincided with the loss of many thousands of managers and technicians. At more or less the same time, the distinct threat of invasion involved diversion of national resources to defense. Thus the typical, newly appointed Cuban manager found himself running a newly created enterprise whose machinery came from a country with which Cuba could no longer trade. The new suppliers and customers were many thousands of miles away and employed completely different trading practices.[5]

The drastic economic transformation resulted in serious production declines, which in turn resulted in severe consumer goods shortages. As the shortages increased, so did popular discontent with Castro, and thousands continued choosing emigration to the United States over economic hardship in Cuba.[6]

Politically, 1961 was also a good time to invade Cuba. Although Castro had been in power for more than two years, his power was not fully consolidated, and a number of well-organized groups still posed a real threat to him. A wide underground network, with strong support from the CIA, was relatively successful in sabotage against the government. In addition, ideological differences within Castro's inner circle had deepened during the two years and continued to do so.

Unfortunately for Kennedy but fortunately for Castro, the timing for the invasion was about the only thing that went according to plan. The 1500-man exile force was defeated in less than seventy-two hours, the Cuban underground network was crushed by massive arrests, and U.S. participation in the invasion was revealed. The operation was such a fiasco that even the president is reported to have commented: "How could I have been so stupid to let them go ahead?"[7]

The Bay of Pigs defeat was Kennedy's most embarrassing foreign policy setback, and he felt personally humiliated by it. Karl E. Meyer and Tad Szulc explain why:

> Invasions had failed before, but seldom had a great power like the United States allowed itself to be caught in so embarrassing a predicament as in the attack on Cuba, mounted, financed, and executed by the Central Intelligence Agency. The military implications of the disaster were obvious: an operation bearing the stamp of approval of the Joint Chiefs of Staff of the world's most powerful nation was destroyed in less than three days by half-trained, part-time militia troops of a disorganized revolutionary state. . . . It was a failure of mind, of imagination, of common sense. . . . It solved nothing, it won nothing.[8]

United States pride and prestige were not the only things affected by the invasion. The operation had profound effects on Fidel Castro and the Cuban revolution's political future, and on the lives of hundreds of thousands of Cubans in exile or anticipating it.

The invasion increased Castro's political power and popularity. Ernesto "Ché" Guevara, Cuba's finance minister, summarized the invasion's effects on Cuba during an informal meeting with White House adviser Richard Goodwin on August 1961:

> Guevara began by asking Goodwin to thank Kennedy for the Bay of Pigs invasion. Before then, he said, Castro had held a tenuous grip on the Cuban Revolution, with the economy in chaos and numerous internal factions plotting against him. But the invasion, Guevara said jovially, had assured Castro's hold on the country. It made him even more of a hero, as the man who had defended Cuba against the greatest power in the world.[9]

The defeated invasion shattered the hopes of 116,000 Cuban exiles in the United States for a quick return to a Cuba without Castro. Within seventy-two hours their options had been reduced to two main choices: (a) to regroup and try another military action under more adverse conditions (the element of surprise had been eliminated, and the Cuban underground network severely damaged) or (b) to come to grips with the grim reality that their exile had been extended for at least a few more years.

While Castro basked in victory by heaping scorn on Kennedy for the invasion, the administration did not give up the idea of overthrowing the revolution. In a secret White House document dated May 3, 1961, less than three weeks after the invasion, a much bigger military program for Cuban exiles was discussed at length:

> The Department of Defense proposes the following terms of reference for the armed services in developing a program of integration of Cuban refugees into a viable armed force. A "Brigade" of 4,000 will be constituted, consisting of approximately 500 Air Force, 500 Navy and 3,000 Army.
>
> Special training could be provided by U.S. Army schools to both individuals and units in the concepts and practice of civil affairs and military government, tailored as necessary to the needs of post-Castro Cuba. . . . Detailed plans are available and would entail the organization of about 500 men into six Civil Affairs units, considered capable of administering the national government in Havana and the other five provinces. [10]

In addition to the long-range military plans for Cuban exiles, the Kennedy administration launched a secret war against Cuba that eventually required the services of several thousand men, and would cost as much $100 million a year. [11]

Kennedy and the Refugees

Like the invasion plans he inherited from the Eisenhower administration, Kennedy also received the refugee strategy planned by his predecessor. On January 18, 1961, the president-elect received Tracy S. Voorhees' report on "The Cuban Refugee Problem."

Voorhees headed Eisenhower's Committee on Hungarian Refugees, and his report on the Cubans reflected his belief that the Cuban operation would be similar to the Hungarian. The operation would pay for itself by anti-Communist propaganda effects alone and would be limited to only a few hundred thousand refugees who would return to Cuba as soon as Castro was overthrown, presumably within a few months or years. The language used in the report is similar to that used by Voorhees in his earlier report on the Hungarians. To him, the Cuban state was another manifestation of Communist oppression, and the United States should respond as it had in 1957:

> This latest exodus of persons fleeing from Communist oppression is the first time in many years in which our nation has become the country of first asylum for any such number of refugees. To grant

such asylum is in accordance with the long-standing tradition of the United States. Our people opened their homes and hearts to the Hungarian refugees four years ago, I am sure we will do no less for the distressed Cubans.[12]

Accepting the recommendations in the Voorhees report, the president ordered the establishment of a Cuban Refugee Program under the Department of Health, Education, and Welfare. The new federal program would do the following:

1. Provide all possible assistance to voluntary relief agencies in providing daily necessities for many of the refugees, for resettling as many as possible, and for securing jobs for them.
2. Obtain the assistance of both private and governmental agencies to provide useful employment opportunities for displaced Cubans, consistent with the overall employment situation prevailing in Florida.
3. Provide supplemental funds for the resettlement of refugees in other areas, including transportation and adjustment costs to the new communities and for their eventual return to Miami for repatriation to their homeland as soon as that is again possible.
4. Furnish financial assistance to meet basic maintenance requirements of needy Cuban refugee families in the Miami area as required in communities of resettlement, administered through Federal, State, and local channels and based on standards used in the community involved.
5. Provide for essential health services through the financial assistance program supplemented by child health, public health services, and other arrangements as needed.
6. Furnish Federal assistance for local public school operating costs related to the unforeseen impact of Cuban refugee children on local teaching facilities.
7. Initiate needed measures to augment training and educational opportunities for Cuban refugees, including, physicians, teachers, and those with other professional backgrounds.
8. Provide financial aid for the care and protection of unaccompanied children—the most defenseless and troubled group among the refugee population.
9. Undertake a surplus food distribution program to be administered by the county welfare department, with surplus foods distributed by public and voluntary agencies to needy refugees.[13]

Direct federal assistance to Cuban exiles had started in December 1960, through the Cuban Refugee Emergency Center in Miami. The new program represented a commitment on a much larger scale and wider scope than ever before. In addition, the resettlement plan outlined in the program indicates that the Cuban migration was already larger than anyone had anticipated, and it was time to do something about it.

The U.S. and Cuban governments used the Cuban Refugee Program to launch political attacks on each other. While lauding Health, Education, and Welfare's Secretary Abraham Ribicoff, President Kennedy noted the program's importance in the fight against communism:

> I also want to commend Secretary Ribicoff for the constructive, humanitarian, and immediate program to assist the Cuban refugees. He said that he hoped that it would be considered first and foremost an essential humanitarian act by this country. But he also wanted it to indicate the resolve of this nation to help those in need who stand with the United States for personal freedom and against Communist penetration of the Western Hemisphere.[14]

Castro, on the other hand, interpreted the Cuban Refugee Program as another threat to his government, and as a justification for Cuban revolutionary activities in Latin America:

> If the United States has the right to approve credit for the Cuban counter-revolutionary exiles, Cuba will approve a credit to help all the Puerto Rican revolutionaries. . . . If the United States has the right to promote a counter-revolution in Cuba, Cuba believes it has the right to promote a revolution in Latin America.[15]

Castro's interpretation of Kennedy's motives sounded too strong for many but, according to Lourdes Arguelles, a Cuban exile sociologist, his reasoning was not without foundation. She argues that the Cuban Refugee Program was central to Kennedy's plans to overthrow the Cuban revolution:

> Although started by the Eisenhower Administration, Cuban refugee social programming was really the brainchild of the Kennedy presidency. Kennedy was strongly committed to and involved in the ongoing covert war against Cuba. Unlike Eisenhower, however, he saw the refugee programs as part of the continuing operation and decided to use United States power in the form of refugee aid on a far bigger scale than previously. For Kennedy these programs were ideal tools to stimulate Cuban migration further. The outflow, he believed, would undermine the revolution by means of a steady brain drain, as well as by its negative impact on the world image of the revolution.[16]

Kennedy's intentions to use the Cuban exiles as political weapons against Castro were shared by William J. vanden Heuvel, president of the International Rescue Committee, who, in a memorandum to the president titled, "Cuba: Its Refugees and Its Liberation," articulated some measures that would later be adopted by the administration. The ten-page document, dated September 6, 1962, argued that the Cuban refugees were a significant part of any action program chosen against Castro. The refugees were considered a political, physical, and psychological force that could be used to bring about and sustain the "liberation" of their country, that it would be a mistake to overlook the political potential of the refugees. Vanden Huevel pointed out that critical welfare and assistance programs on behalf of the refugees were jeopardized and that the administration should consider the appointment of a director for the Cuban Refugee Program with sufficient White House backing to coordinate the humanitarian and political objectives of the program.[17]

Vanden Heuvel's memorandum to the president also recommended a number of specific political and military actions to be carried out against Castro:

> By concentrating the spotlight on the refugees and the 50,000 political prisoners in Castro's jails, we would remind the world that another Police State has been created which is capable of all the torture and brutality which this century has symbolized. . . . The refugees provide us with an opportunity to deal with legitimate Cuban interests and to develop a striking force capable of sustained guerrilla action against Castro. . . . The imaginative and creative forces in America which are capable of waging succesful political warfare must be galvanized. In that effort, reconsideration of the refugees' significance will be crucial.[18]

The Kennedy administration's strategy to drain Cuba of its best qualified professionals had a devastating short-term effect on the Cuban economy. In addition to shortages of consumer goods and the general economic dislocations exacerbated by the departure of thousands of technicians, the flight of thousands of physicians seriously damaged Castro's plan to expand rural medical facilities.[19] The exodus became so large, and its effects so damaging, that the Cuban government tried to stop the fleeing professionals by depriving them of their citizenship and prohibiting their return to their families in Cuba. When these measures failed to stem the tide, however, Castro tried to downplay the exodus, dismissing it as a misguided and mistaken decision that the exiles would some day regret: "When they get fed up with Yankeeism and tired of being despised and mistreated, when they get tired of the idiosyncracies of their imperialist masters, the day will come when they will knock on our door asking to be let in."[20]

Raúl Castro also tried to downplay the flight of professionals. He believed, however, that the exodus was a natural purification process that actually strengthened the revolution:

> Those who go are inept or unadaptable to the new life. Those involved in counterrevolutionary activities are really few. . . . It is the normal exodus that takes place when the people take the power in their own hands and liquidate exploitation and the privileged classes. Their departure does not damage the revolution but fortifies it, as it is a spontaneous purification.[21]

Fidel and Raúl Castro were both right, for the general exodus of disaffected Cubans had a paradoxical dual effect. On one hand, the departures hurt the revolution because the urgently needed professionals could not be replaced fast enough—with either native or foreign talent—to prevent economic disruptions and human suffering. On the other hand, the departure of a large part of the political and economic elite made Castro's political consolidation easier and faster.

Amid the political war between the U.S. and Cuban governments, Cuban refugees continued to arrive in Miami in record numbers. In 1961 more than 33,000 arrived, more than in 1959 and 1960 combined.[22] In addition, the United States embassy in Havana had issued more than 20,000 visas and visa-waivers to Cubans with relatives in the United States. But, because the Cuban government required payment in dollars for flights to Miami, those eligible to leave were momentarily stranded for lack of money.

The Kennedy administration responded to the crisis by offering a free airlift from Cuba starting in August 1961, at a cost of $350,000 to the United States. The president also sent a bill to Congress calling for $10 million a year to meet "unexpected refugee migration problems," and reminded the Congress that "this country has always served as a lantern in the dark for those who love freedom but are persecuted, in misery, or in need."[23]

The $10 million was a large sum, considering that it represented an increase of more than 100 percent from the Cuban Refugee Program's initial budget of $4 million in February 1961. By 1962, however, the program's operating budget would rise to $38 million a year, and continue rising steadily until it reached a high of $136 million in 1972.[24] But money was not a problem as long as the program achieved its goals, especially that of resettling as many refugees as possible away from the Miami area.

Resettlement was not only one of the program's main priorities, but its biggest success. According to Cuban Refugee Program figures, of 447,795 refugees registered with the Center from January 1961 to December 1972, 296,806 were resettled outside Miami.[25] Such a high rate, 66.3 percent, was no small achievement in light of the Cubans' strong reluctance to leave Miami.[26]

While the humanitarian aspects of the Cuban Refugee Program worked according to plan, resettling more than half the Cuban exile population outside Miami and providing financial aid and medical care for all who needed it, the political aspects did not. But the administration never gave up its hopes that the refugees would figure somehow in the overthrow of Castro and the formation of a pro-United States regime.

In a secret memorandum of July 1963, George C. Denney, Jr., the State Department's director of intelligence and research, outlined a number of possible courses of action against Cuba. These included plans to involve other Latin American nations with a view to overthrowing Castro. The memorandum argued that the United States should try to:

> Reverse the present David-Goliath relationship with Cuba by having a smaller and militarily helpless Central American state, with a highly respected leader, engage Castro in a propaganda struggle in order to distract Castro and provoke him into threatening and unwise countermoves. If successful, the plan would: 1) make an ordinary bully out of a heroically posturing Castro, cause him to lose self-esteem, and possibly involve him in a chain reaction of mistakes, 2) increase Latin American concern over Cuban subversion and promote OAS cooperation in defense of a small nation (the US should be the last to interfere overtly), 3) provide the US with an excuse to take further action against Cuba, should such escalation become desirable, and 4) present a Cuba-obsessed American public opinion with a new outlook on a Castro cut down to smaller dimensions.[27]

Denney's memorandum, dated July 25, chose to ignore the fact that the missile crisis of October 1962 was settled by an agreement between the United States and the Soviet Union in which the United States promised to keep its hands off Cuba.[28] There is no indication that Kennedy contemplated a second invasion or other direct military or political action against Cuba in violation of the agreement with the Soviet Union.[29]

Whatever his political motivations, John F. Kennedy must be credited with launching the largest, longest-running, and most expensive aid program for refugees from Latin America ever undertaken by the United States. During its fifteen-year history, the Cuban Refugee Program aided more than 700,000 Cubans, at a cost of more than a billion dollars to the U.S. government. The president failed to overthrow Castro, but his generous program for refugees from Cuba remains unequaled.

Notes

1. Hugh Sidey, *John F. Kennedy, President* (New York, 1963), 34. For more on Kennedy's philosophy and ideals, see Arthur M. Schlesinger, Jr., *A Thousand Days: John F. Kennedy in the White House* (Boston, 1965); and Theodore C. Sorensen, *Kennedy* (New York, 1965). For a more detached and critical treatment of the Kennedy administration, see Henry Fairlie, *The Kennedy Promise: The Politics of Expectation* (New York, 1973); and Herbert S. Parmet, *The Presidency of John F. Kennedy* (New York, 1983).

2. *U.S. News and World Report*, January 16, 1961, 38. For more details on Kennedy's position on Cuba during the campaign, and more statements on Castro, see Theodore H. White, *The Making of the President 1960* (New York, 1961).

3. For more on McCarthyism's impact on U.S. politics and foreign policy, see Richard H. Rovere, *Senator Joe McCarthy* (New York, 1959); and Lawrence S. Wittner, *Cold War America: From Hiroshima to Watergate* (New York, 1974).

4. *U.S. News and World Report*, January 16, 1961, 38.

5. Robin Blackburn, "The Economics of the Cuban Revolution," in Nelson Goodsell, ed., *Fidel Castro's Personal Revolution*, 143.

6. Richard R. Fagen, Richard A. Brody, and Thomas J. O'Leary, *Cubans in Exile: Disaffection and the Revolution* (Stanford, 1968).

7. Peter Wyden, *Bay of Pigs: The Untold Story* (New York, 1979), 8. For more on the CIA's role in the invasion, see Howard E. Hunt, *Give Us This Day* (New Rochelle, 1973); and David Wise and Thomas B. Ross, *The Invisible Government* (New York, 1964).

8. Karl Meyer and Tad Szulc, *The Cuban Invasion* (New York, 1962), 77. The Bay of Pigs invasion has been the subject of many books and articles. In addition to the sources previously cited, the following are also useful: Haynes Johnson, *The Bay of Pigs: The Leaders' Story* (New York, 1964); Irving L. Janis, "A Perfect

Failure: The Bay of Pigs," in *Victims of Group Think: A Psychological Study of Foreign Policy Decisions and Fiascos* (Boston, 1972); Rafael del Pino, *Amanecer en Girón* (Havana, 1961); and David A. Phillips, *The Night Watch* (New York, 1977).

9. Taylor Branch and George Crile, III, "The Kennedy Vendetta: How the CIA Waged a Silent War Against Cuba," *Harper's*, August 1975, 61.

10. U.S. Policy Toward Cuban Exiles, 3 May 1961, Theodore C. Sorensen Papers, John F. Kennedy Library, Boston, Massachussetts.

11. For more on the CIA's operations against Cuba, see Warren Hinckle, *The Fish Is Red: The Story of the Secret War Against Castro* (New York, 1981); Bradley E. Ayers, *The War That Never Was: An Insider's Account of CIA Covert Operations Against Cuba* (Indianapolis, 1976); Thomas Powers, "Inside the Department of Dirty Tricks," *The Atlantic Monthly*, August 1979.

12. *State Department Bulletin*, February 13, 1961, 219.

13. *State Department Bulletin*, February 27, 1961, 309–10.

14. Ibid., 310.

15. *New York Times*, February 12, 1961, 1.

16. Lourdes Arguelles, "Cuban Miami: The Roots, Development, and Every-day Life of an Emigre Enclave in the United States National Security State," *Contemporary Marxism* 5 (Summer 1982): 29–30.

17. William J. vanden Heuvel, Memorandum on Cuba: Its Refugees and Its Liberation, 6 September 1962. File "Classified Subjects," Kennedy Library. This memo was only recently declassified.

18. Ibid., 8–10.

19. One of Castro's main promises to the Cuban people was to improve the deplorable state of medical services in the rural areas. For more on the state of rural medicine before and after the revolution, see Lowry Nelson, *Rural Cuba* (Minneapolis, 1950); Wyatt MacGaffey and Clifford R. Barnett, *Twentieth-Century Cuba: Background of the Castro Revolution* (New York, 1965); Medea Benjamin, Joseph Collins, and Michael Scoll, *No Free Lunch: Food and Revolution in Cuba Today* (San Francisco, 1984).

20. *New York Times*, September 7, 1961, 10.

21. *New York Times*, July 23, 1961, 21.

22. *New York Times*, April 12, 1962, 14.

23. *Newsweek*, July 31, 1961, 7.

24. Rafael Prohías and Lourdes Casal, "The Cuban Minority in the United States: Preliminary Report on Need Identification and Program Evaluation" (Washington D.C., 1974), 104.

25. Ibid., 108.

26. Most people interviewed for this study resisted resettlement from Miami because they believed that Castro would not last long, and they wanted to be near Cuba to return as soon as possible. Others, my family included, refused resettlement because they preferred Miami's large Cuban community and warm weather.

27. George C. Denney, Jr., Memorandum on Cuba: "Possible Courses of Action," 25 July 1963. Kennedy Papers, File "National Security," Kennedy Library.

28. For details on the missile crisis and the negotiations that led to its settlement, see Abram Chayes, *The Cuban Missile Crisis. International Crisis and the Role of Law* (New York, 1974); Graham T. Allison, *Essence of Decision: Explaining the Cuban Missile Crisis* (Boston, 1971); Robert F. Kennedy, *Thirteen*

Days: A Memoir of the Cuban Missile Crisis (New York, 1969); Schlesinger, *A Thousand Days*; Sorensen, *Kennedy*.

29. Kennedy's efforts to overthrow Castro present an interesting irony. Although he was by far the most active anti-Castro U.S. president, in terms of covert and overt actions against Cuba, many exiles seriously believe he was a "leftist" or "Communist." The main reason for the misconception is Kennedy's failure with the Bay of Pigs invasion. Cuban exiles argue that if the president had provided adequate air cover for the invading forces, the operation would have succeeded. Thus they feel betrayed. For more on the "Cuba Betrayed" theory, see Lazo, *Dagger in the Heart*.

5

The Camarioca Boatlift and the Airlift of 1965 to 1973

I declare this afternoon to the people of Cuba that those who seek refuge here in America will find it. The dedication of America to our tradition as an asylum for the oppressed is going to be upheld.

Lyndon B. Johnson, October 3, 1965

The Announcement

ON SEPTEMBER 28, 1965, before a large crowd in Havana's Plaza de la Revolución, Fidel Castro surprised everyone with the announcement that Cubans with relatives in the United States could leave the island, if their relatives asked for them.[1] Castro rationalized his decision by blaming the United States for cutting normal avenues of exit from Cuba following the October 1962 missile crisis: "Now they [those wishing to leave Cuba] are leaving in small boats, many of them drowning . . . and they [the Americans] use this as propaganda. . . . Now those who want to leave can because there are many here remaining who struggle for the people. . . . Now we should see what the imperialists will do or say."[2]

Castro's words carried implicit political messages for the Cuban people and the Johnson administration. It was time for Cubans to take sides: those who were not willing to "struggle for the people" were encouraged to take advantage of the offer and leave the country. For the United States it was time to define its immigration policy toward Cuba. Beginning October 10, boats from Miami—most piloted by Cuban exiles—would be welcomed at the port of

Camarioca to pick up their relatives. What happened when these boats returned to Florida was the United States' problem.

The administration's initial reaction to Castro's announcement was cautious and somewhat skeptical but also positive. The State Department said it was studying the proposal carefully, but made it clear that the Cubans would undoubtedly be admitted to the United States if they were permitted to leave the island. The State Department also pointed out that "policy always has been to admit bona fide refugees from Communist oppression."[3]

To erase any doubts expressed by U.S. officials and to show that he was serious, Castro on September 30 strengthened his original proposal by offering two flights daily from Havana to Miami. He implied that the flights would be free.[4] So Castro was not only serious, but determined to send a new wave of Cubans to the United States.

Almost overnight, and without warning, the Cuban government presented the United States with a refugee crisis. Unlike the gradual and orderly flow of Cuban refugees into Florida of the previous six years, the Camarioca boatlift portended disaster. The open-homes-and-hearts policy was being challenged, and the administration searched for a proper response.

From January 1959 to October 1960, only 10,000 Cubans sought asylum in the United States. They consisted mainly of members of the richest families in Cuba affected by Castro's agrarian reform. The number increased to 56,000 in 1961, this time composed largely of professionals and technicians. The largest wave came between October 1961 and October 1962, at which time the flow was temporarily stopped as a result of the Cuban missile crisis. Since then, another 45,000 had entered the United States, but at a much slower pace than during the preceding years.[5] This flow of Cubans averaged only 35,000 a year, a small enough number to allow for a relatively normal immigration procedure.[6]

The prospect of more than 200,000 refugees coming in during a short period of time represented a legitimate cause of alarm for the Johnson administration. Castro's proposal would, in just a few months, almost double the number of Cuban refugees in the United States from 211,000 to 411,000 (see Table 5.1).[7]

Why Camarioca?

Castro's announcement seemed to have caught most American analysts and policy makers by surprise. The key question was

---

Table 5.1   Waves of Cuban Immigration, 1961–1972

1. January 1961 to the Missile Crisis of October 1962   153,534
2. November 1962 to November 1965   29,962
3. December 1965 to March 1972   277,242

Source: Darrell Lynn Bender, "Cuban Exiles: An Analytical Sketch," *Journal of Latin American Studies* 5, part 2 (November 1973): 272.

---

why Castro adopted the policy, and American experts searched for answers. Castro repeated his original argument, but offered little additional information other than that of his September 28 speech: "right after the missile crisis of October 1962, the United States Government canceled daily flights between the United States and Cuba and refused to reopen them despite Cuba's protest."[8] More interesting and portentous, however, was Castro's explanation of the Johnson administration's political motives to accept the new refugees: "The U.S.A. uses emigration from Cuba as a political weapon. . . . if before the Revolution the United States had permitted free entrance of Cuban citizens without restriction, a much larger number would have gone then than the total of all who have left since the Revolution or who will in the future."[9] Castro also emphasized the special status refugees from revolutionary Cuba enjoyed vis-à-vis other Latin American countries: "To what other underdeveloped country in this hemisphere has the United States offered its citizens an opportunity to immigrate freely? Any other Latin American country to which it made such an offer would empty out overnight."[10]

Although Castro's assertions were obviously exaggerated and only partially explained the external dimension of the situation, he was fairly accurate in his speculations about the problems the United States' use of immigration policy as a political weapon could create if other nations were to become involved. Such a scenario became reality in the late 1970s and early 1980s when the United States faced simultaneous refugee influxes from Cuba, Haiti, Nicaragua, Guatemala, and El Salvador (see Chapter 8), as well as economically motivated migrations from the entire Caribbean Basin region.

Although Castro blamed the United States for the new influx, he ignored Cuba's internal political and economic situation in his pronouncements. The United States mass media, however, wasted little time offering speculative explanations. According to *U.S. News and World Report*, Castro had three main reasons for allowing thousands to leave: (1) to open talks with the United States ultimately leading to normalized diplomatic relations between the United States and Cuba; (2) to ease internal problems by eliminating nonproductive Cubans (men of military age 14 to 27 were not permitted to leave); and (3) to provide a safety valve by letting dissidents go to the United States.[11] Similar theories were also advanced by the *New York Times*, *Time* Magazine, and the *Miami Herald*.[12]

In a secret report written more than a year before Castro's announcement, the Central Intelligence Agency assessed Cuba's internal situation as marked by growing popular discontent with the government and economy. The document pointed to the institution of obligatory military service, the confiscation of all remaining private farms larger than 167 acres, and the system of standardized wages for all nonagricultural workers, as the leading causes for antigovernment feelings.[13] If the CIA's assessment was accurate, most people wishing to emigrate to the United States when the opportunity presented itself seemed to be disaffected because of the economic situation and not political repression.

Nonetheless, President Johnson chose to explain the new refugee influx strictly in political terms. In his first public reaction to Castro's proposal, the president went to Ellis Island, New York, to sign the Immigration Bill. Standing under the shadow of the Statue of Liberty, the president declared that the United States would welcome the refugees with the thought that "in another day, they can return to their homeland to find it cleansed of terror and free from fear."[14]

The president's emphasis on the "terror" and "fear" that the refugees presumably experienced in their homeland had an immediate impact on the media's views. The day following Johnson's statement, the *Miami Herald* editorialized:

> Offering sanctuary to victims of persecution in other lands is traditional for the United States. The open door has been busy since Fidel Castro and his Communist handlers sneaked into power in Cuba nearly seven years ago. Now we are about to receive thousands more fugitives from the captive island 90 miles from our shores.[15]

Johnson's declarations and executive actions opened the gates to all Cubans "escaping from Communism." Like Eisenhower before him, the president perceived the Cuban migration as a short-term emergency rather than a process with long-range implications not only for refugees from Cuba, but all of Latin America and the developing world. The president's decision to allow the boatlift from Cuba set the tone for United States immigration policy for at least the next fifteen years, when new crises would again have to be solved in the absence of a clearly defined policy.

The Crisis Unfolds

While Castro and Johnson blamed one another for the new migration, October 10 arrived and the human traffic began its perilous movement across the Florida straits. Hundreds of vessels of all sizes arrived at the Port of Camarioca, and as promised, were allowed to pick up relatives and friends. Only normal delays and complications occurred.[16]

The boatlift proceeded with relative speed and calm despite the rough hurricane-season weather and heavy seas. In fact, the threatening weather was largely responsible for the premature cancellation of the operation after only 5,000 of the estimated 200,000 had arrived in Florida.[17]

As the boatlift grew more dangerous, negotiations to end it and to establish a safer and more orderly passage intensified. Castro repeatedly rejected Johnson's proposal to have the International Red Cross assist the refugees. He argued that the Swiss Embassy, which represented United States interests in Cuba, was sufficient. Ambassador Emil Stadelhofer, in a seven-hour meeting at a Havana Pizzeria, negotiated with Castro to secure new rules for migration from Cuba to the United States.[18]

Ambassador Stadelhofer's efforts set the stage for a formal agreement establishing procedures and means for the movement of Cuban refugees to the United States. Some of the most important provisions outlined in the "Memorandum of Understanding" signed by the United States and Cuba on November 6, 1965, were:

1. The Government of Cuba agrees to permit the departure from Cuba of, and the Government of the United States agrees to permit the entry into the United States of, Cubans who wish to leave Cuba for the United States.
2. Persons living in Cuba who are immediate relatives of persons now living in the United States will be given, as a group, first priority in processing and movement.

3. The Government of the United States agrees to provide air transportation to carry persons permitted to depart Cuba and to enter the United States from Varadero [70 miles East of Havana] to a point in the United States [Miami].
4. The Government of the United States agrees to provide transportation with such frequency and capacity as to permit the movement of between 3,000 and 4,000 persons per month.
5. The two Governments agree that the first movement under the terms of this memorandum of understanding will begin not later than December 1, 1965.[19]

Attempting to avoid past mistakes, the Cuban government placed strict qualifications for exit permits. Men of military age, 14 through 27, could not take advantage of the airlift. Neither could persons "whose departure might produce grave disturbance to production or to a social service because of the lack of a replacement."[20]

News of the new agreement triggered powerful reactions in both Cuba and the United States. In Cuba tens of thousands applied for exit permits at the risk of losing their jobs and properties and being labeled "counterrevolutionaries," "worms," and "antisocials." Cuban communities in the United States rejoiced as thousands anxiously awaited the family reunifications the new airlift promised. Spanish-language radio stations were flooded with calls from Cuban exiles willing to help the new immigrants with jobs, housing, clothing, and food.[21]

In addition to the tremendous outpouring of happiness and human cooperation expressed by Cuban exile communities over family reunification, a strong political factor was at work. The idea of two daily flights of "refugees from communism" in "freedom flights," as they were soon popularly dubbed, represented a propaganda victory over Castro for both the Cuban exiles and the Johnson administration.

The federally arranged migration of 4,000 refugees a month, however, alarmed and outraged some Florida officials and many in Miami.[22] Newspapers and broadcasting stations received hundreds of phone calls objecting to the airlift agreement. Governor Haydon Burns and Miami Mayor Robert King High publicly predicted economic chaos unless there was massive relocation of refugees outside of Florida and considerable federal help to the local areas.[23]

The group that felt most threatened by the new refugees was the Miami black community. In a letter to President Johnson,

Donald Wheeler Jones, president of the Miami Beach Branch of the National Association for the Advancement of Colored People, outlined his group's fears:

> A cursory observation of the employment patterns of many Miami and Miami Beach hotels, restaurants, and other businesses will substantiate the fact that the Cuban has displaced the Negro and other personnel formerly employed there in many capacities such as waiters, bell-hops, doormen, elevator operators, and other similar occupations. There are many other categories of employment, almost too numerous to mention, that Negroes no longer enjoy as a direct result of the Cuban influx which apparently is about to be extended. In short, the Cuban influx of immigrants to this country have had their most severe effect upon that group of citizens least able to afford it, the uneducated, non-highly skilled, non-professional Negro, who prior to the Cuban influx could eke out a fairly decent standard of living through menial, service type jobs that require a minimum of formal education or training. [24]

Jones's assessment was proved correct just a few weeks later when Buford Ellington, presidential aide in charge of the Office of Emergency Planning, discovered that unemployment in Miami was less than 5 percent among Cubans and 13 to 17 percent among blacks. [25]

Tensions between blacks and Cubans, however, had deeper roots and more serious consequences than the groups' disparate unemployment rates. Among the many complaints blacks had against the refugees was that blacks, as American citizens, were not getting governmental assistance comparable to the quantity and quality of that given to the refugees. Blacks also complained that Cuban children were integrated into the public schools while blacks remained segregated, that the federal government relief subsidy was greater for the refugees than the local relief for black indigents, and that job placement activities for refugees allegedly resulted in blacks losing jobs traditionally held open primarily for them (such as bellmen, porters, and chambermaids). [26] These legitimate complaints underlined not only the inherent racism of American society, but the glaring contradictions between the Cuban immigration policy and Johnson's Great Society program.

The new Cuban influx threatened to exacerbate further an already tense racial situation in south Florida. There were even rumors that another black uprising like that in the Los Angeles community of Watts would occur if the refugees came. In addition, extremist groups like the John Birch Society sought to exploit the racial tensions by inflaming anti-Cuban feelings among the white population.[27]

Black-Cuban tension was not the only issue raised by the hundreds who voiced their opinions against the refugees.[28] One major concern was over the refugees' "legitimacy." Were they really fleeing communism or were they spies? Some even questioned the president's wisdom and judgment. These concerns were clearly and emphatically addressed by A. C. Adams, who reversed the ideological color normally ascribed to the refugees in an impassioned letter to the president:

> Why should the immigration laws be set aside to invite Communists here from Cuba? It appears to be a great opportunity for the Communists to come into the United States and commit sabotage and to stir up racial trouble and other kinds of strife. Or are we all so naive as to believe that no Communists will be sent here from Cuba? . . . As long as we are at war with the Communists on the other side of the world, it appears foolish and ridiculous to befriend them here at our front door.[29]

Adams's skepticism was counterbalanced by those who saw a positive side to the massive refugee influx. United States Representative Claude Pepper (Democrat of Florida) lauded the president's decision because he believed Cubans were a good source of cheap labor.[30] A more ambitious plan was proposed by J. A. Gore, who suggested that the United States, working through the Organization of American States, should scatter the refugees throughout Latin America. In this way, all countries in the hemisphere "would hear the truth from these Cubans about life under Communism."[31] Amid such fervent debate, the Cuban airlift began as scheduled on December 1, 1965.

The Cuban Airlift

The agreement to establish a regular air bridge between Cuba and the United States did not signal a thaw in relations between the two countries. The Johnson administration made it clear that "the United States did not intend to abandon its policy of trying to isolate Cuba." Johnson saw the agreement as part of the promise he had made to the Cuban people on October 3.[32]

The administration was willing to solve the immediate crisis, but not the underlying problem of Cuban immigration. To negotiate a long-range policy with the Cuban government could have been perceived as weakness instead of strength. Thus immigration from Cuba would remain in limbo until the next crisis.

As expected, the airlift or "freedom flights" provided sensational headlines and human interest stories for the mass media. The *Miami Herald* and the *New York Times* reported on the airlift at least weekly throughout its duration.[33] Other national publications like *Time, Newsweek*, and *U.S. News and World Report* also reported the flights regularly, but unlike the *Herald* and the *Times*, those publications concentrated on the political aspects of the airlift and its damage to the Cuban government, instead of the real human drama being played out twice a day, five days a week at Miami's International Airport.[34] The Cuban press, on the other hand, reported the airlift as nothing extraordinary. Regular reports on the flights were soon relegated to the back pages of *Granma, Juventud Rebelde*, and *Bohemia*. Almost systematically, however, derogatory terms such as "gusano" (worm) were used to describe those who opted for exile in the United States over life in revolutionary Cuba.[35]

During its first year, the Cuban airlift brought more than 45,000 refugees to Miami. In a press release marking the anniversary, Health, Education, and Welfare Secretary John W. Gardner declared that the operation was working as planned. The secretary was particularly happy that families had been reunited. Of the 8,600 children sent alone to the United States by their parents from 1959 to 1965, only 420 still needed care in foster homes and institutions. Gardner also praised the refugees' lack of need for government financial help: "As in the past, only about five percent of resettled refugees require Federal assistance and usually only for a short period of time."[36]

Florida officials viewed the situation much differently than Secretary Gardner. Governor Burns was worried at estimates of more than 700,000 Cubans waiting to fly to the United States, since most Cubans preferred to stay in Miami: their families resided there, south Florida's climate is similar to Cuba's, and knowledge of English was not necessary for survival. The Miami community continued its public debate over the "flood of refugees" and its adverse effects on South Florida's economy. Refugees became the primary topic on radio talk shows and in letters to the editors of Florida's major newspapers. Nonetheless, the flights continued and so did the resettlement program, which placed Cubans in 2,100 communities in every state of the union. Of the 224,000 refugees registered with the U.S. Cuban Refugee Center in Miami since 1961, some 131,000 had been resettled outside the Miami area.[37] Even so, by 1969 more than 25 percent of the new refugees were settling in Miami.[38]

The Johnson administration tried to satisfy Miami officials and the general public by allocating more federal funds for the airlift and related expenses. On June 28, 1968, Johnson authorized the transfer of up to $1.8 million from the Foreign Assistance Program to the Department of Health, Education, and Welfare "in order for that agency to meet unexpected urgent refugee and migration needs arising in connection with assistance to Cuban refugees in the United States" (see Table 5.2).[39]

By the time Johnson left the White House in January 1969, the Cuban airlift and relocation program were costing more than $100 million a year, and after three years of flights, the end was nowhere in sight. The memorandum of understanding between Cuba and the United States specified how and when the refugees would come to the United States, but it said nothing about how many or for how long.

Richard Nixon inherited the Cuban airlift in 1969 and, like his predecessor, had to find ways of transferring funds from different federal programs in order to cope with the rising cost of the influx.[40] During the Nixon administration, the cost of the program triggered heated debates in Congress, where sentiment was running high in favor of cutting funds. With a price tag of $120 million a year in 1970, some in Congress even tried to shift airlift funds to the urban poor in the United States.[41] This move was narrowly defeated after administration officials testified that the flights "are their [Cubans] only hope to escape from Communism."[42]

The flights were not going smoothly either. A number of short, temporary cancellations had marred the program since the late 1960s. Once again, the two governments blamed each other for the problems. Cuba claimed that the United States was "dragging its feet" in processing refugee permits, and that the list of those willing to emigrate was about to be exhausted.[43] The United States

**Table 5.2   Geographical Distribution of Resettled Cuban Refugees
(June 1961 to December 30, 1966)**

State	Number of refugees	State	Number of refugees
Alabama	286	Montana	144
Alaska	1	Nebraska	363
Arizona	150	Nevada	7,003
Arkansas	64	New Hampshire	93
California	14,194	New Jersey	19,953
Colorado	1,032	New Mexico	312
Connecticut	1,627	New York	37,345
Delaware	220	North Carolina	352
District of Columbia	1,546	North Dakota	45
Florida	3,529	Ohio	1,583
Georgia	1,150	Oklahoma	457
Hawaii	26	Oregon	559
Idaho	4	Pennsylvania	2,356
Illinois	8,662	Rhode Island	286
Indiana	9,938	South Carolina	199
Iowa	418	South Dakota	48
Kansas	680	Tennessee	400
Kentucky	253	Texas	3,243
Louisiana	2,727	Utah	13
Maine	22	Vermont	41
Maryland	764	Virginia	1,341
Massachusetts	4,394	Washington	306
Michigan	1,339	West Virginia	141
Minnesota	371	Wisconsin	500
Mississippi	94	Wyoming	15
Missouri	860		

Puerto Rico: 13,323; Virgin Islands: 39; 26 Foreign Countries: 908
Total persons resettled from June 1961 to December 30, 1966: 130,599

Source: Cuban Refugee Center, Miami, Florida, Statistical Unit. Reproduced in John F. Thomas, "Cuban Refugees in the United States," *International Migration Review*, vol. 1, 52.

claimed that Cuba wanted to halt the flight of persons with needed skills and professional training.[44]

Despite the charges and countercharges, the flights continued, as did opposition to them in the United States. Miamians insisted that the cost was too high in monetary and social terms. They claimed that the steady influx of Cubans was altering Miami's ethnic character and creating economic problems.[45] Even Senator Edward Kennedy, a long-time supporter of the Cuban Refugee Program, criticized the hasty resettlement program for "creating more problems for all involved." He urged that aid be supplied through regular federal government programs instead of through the special Cuban office administered by the Department of Health, Education, and Welfare.[46] As the airlift entered its seventh year (1972) and exceeded the 250,000-passenger mark, its future looked extremely uncertain.

On April 6, 1973, Eastern Airlines flight 8894 touched down at Miami International Airport at 11:55 A.M. with the last eighty-four passengers of the Cuban airlift. Since 1965, 3,049 flights had brought 260,561 Cubans to the United States, making the Cuban airlift the largest airborne refugee operation in American history.[47]

The Camarioca boatlift and the subsequent airlift were undertaken in the absence of a clear immigration policy for refugees from Cuba. Both operations were perceived as emergencies and handled as such. Neither Johnson nor Nixon tried to normalize the immigration policy during the airlift's seven years. Funds, transportation, employment, food, medical care, and shelter were made available according to the flow of refugees. In the meantime, immigration reform would have to wait.

Notes

1. "Why Castro Exports Cubans," *New York Times Magazine*, November 7, 1965, 30.

2. *New York Times*, September 30, 1965, 1; *Miami Herald*, September 29, 1965, 1a.

3. *New York Times*, September 30, 1965, 2. The *Miami Herald* called Castro's offer a "propaganda bomb" (September 30, 6a). For more reactions to the offer, including the Cuban community's and other Miami leaders', see *Miami Herald*, September 30, 1965, 1a, and October 2, 1965, 1a.

4. *New York Times*, October 1, 1965, 2.

5. *New York Times*, November 7, 1965, 130.

6. Lourdes Casal, "Cubans in the United States: Their Impact on U.S.-Cuban Relations," in Martin Weinstein, ed.; *Revolutionary Cuba in the World Arena* (Philadelphia, 1979), 111.

7. Ibid.

8. Lee Lockwood, *Castro's Cuba, Cuba's Fidel* (New York, 1967), 290.

9. Ibid., 291. The Cuban media consistently repeated Castro's "official" explanation for the Camarioca decision. See *Granma*, October 1–10, 1965.

10. Lockwood, *Castro's Cuba*, 291.

11. *U.S. News and World Report*, November 8, 1965, 50.

12. See *New York Times Magazine*, November 7, 1965, 30–31, and *Time* Magazine, October 15, 1965, 51.

13. Central Intelligence Agency, "Survey of Latin America," vol. 1, 77–78, Johnson Library, Austin, Texas.

14. *Miami Herald*, October 4, 1965, 1a.

15. *Miami Herald*, October 5, 1965, 6a. See also *New York Times*, October 5, 1965, 1.

16. The sea traffic between Cuba and the Florida Keys was covered extensively by the *Miami Herald* and the *New York Times* between October 9 and December 1, 1965. Major periodicals also provided ample coverage but with an emphasis on the sensational. For example, *Newsweek* called the boatlift an "exodus" and "another Dunkirk" (November 1, 1965, 54, and October 18, 1965, 48).

17. Because the boatlift was not regulated and often chaotic, no one really knows how many people drowned or otherwise lost their lives during the eight weeks of sea traffic, but it is estimated that at least several dozen people perished. See *New York Times*, October 31, 1965, 1, and November 4, 1965, 1.

18. *Time* Magazine, November 5, 1965, 56.

19. For the full text of the agreement, see *State Department Bulletin*, November 29, 1965, 850–53.

20. Ibid., 252; *New York Times*, October 24, 1965, 1.

21. *New York Times*, November 7, 1965, 60.

22. *Time* Magazine, November 12, 1965, 36.

23. *St. Petersburg Times*, December 5, 1965, 4d. Governor Burns made his views known to President Johnson even before the memorandum of understanding was signed. In a letter to the president dated October 5, 1965, Burns outlined the role of the federal government in easing the refugee flow. Haydon Burns to Lyndon B. Johnson, 5 October 1965, File "National Security-Defense," Johnson Library.

24. Donald Wheeler Jones to Lyndon B. Johnson, 13 October 1965, File "National Security-Defense," Johnson Library.

25. Buford Ellington, Memorandum on Cuban Refugees, 3 November 1965, File "National Security-Defense," Johnson Library.

26. Seymour Samet, Memorandum on Growing Negro-Cuban Tensions, 19 October 1965, Johnson Papers, File "National Security-Defense," Johnson Library.

27. Harold T. Hunton, Memorandum on Growing Negro-Cuban Tensions, 19 October 1965, Johnson Papers, File "National Security-Defense," Johnson Library.

28. *Time* reported that "newspapers and broadcasting stations received hundreds of letters and phone calls objecting to the new influx of immigrants"; *Time* Magazine, November 12, 1965, 36. See also *Miami Herald*, October 5, 1965, 1b; *New York Times*, November 21, 1965, 3; and *Business Week*, October 16, 1965, 30–31.

29. A. C. Adams to Lyndon B. Johnson, 26 October 1965, File "National Security-Defense," Johnson Library.

30. Claude Pepper to Lyndon B. Johnson, 1 November 1965, File "National Security-Defense," Johnson Library.

31. J. A. Gore to Paul Rogers, 5 October 1965, File "National Security-Defense," Johnson Library.

32. *New York Times*, November 7, 1965, 1. Since 1961, the United States practiced a policy that effectively isolated the island nation economically and politically from most of the Western Hemisphere. See Lynn Darrell Bender, *The Politics of Hostility: Castro's Revolution and United States Policy* (Hato Rey, Puerto Rico, 1975).

33. See *Miami Herald* and *New York Times* from December 1, 1965, to April 7, 1973.

34. For a series of articles that come close to exploiting the situation in the name of sensationalism, with titles such as "Exodus by Air," "Freedom Flood," "Fly Now," "Why Cubans Want to Escape," see *Time* Magazine, *Newsweek*, and *U.S. News and World Report* between December 1, 1965, and April 7, 1973.

35. See *Granma*, *Juventud Rebelde*, and *Bohemia*, December 1, 1965, to April 7, 1973.

36. Philip A. Holman, Press Release on the Cuban Airlift, 1 December 1966, File "National Security-Defense," Johnson Library.

37. Ibid.

38. *New York Times*, December 2, 1969, 92.

39. Lyndon B. Johnson, Memorandum on Presidential Determination No. 68, 29 June 1968, Johnson Papers, File "Confidential," Johnson Library.

40. *New York Times*, September 7, 1972, 8.

41. *New York Times*, July 10, 1970, 4.

42. Ibid.

43. See *Granma*, August 9, 1971, 1; September 28, 1971, 3; November 19, 1971, 1.

44. See *New York Times*, September 1, 1971, 10, and September 5, 1971, 5; and *U.S. News and World Report*, September 13, 1971, 91.

45. *New York Times*, September 5, 1971, 58.

46. *New York Times*, January 11, 1972, 12.

47. Lorrin Philipson and Rafael Llerena, *Freedom Flights* (New York, 1980), 197.

6

Mariel: The Open Door in Crisis

We will continue to provide an open heart and open arms to refugees seeking freedom from Communist domination.

Jimmy Carter, May 5, 1980

United States–Cuba Relations Under Carter

WHEN JIMMY CARTER BECAME PRESIDENT of the United States on January 20, 1977, a new era in U.S.–Cuba relations seemed to be dawning. On January 31, Secretary of State Cyrus Vance declared that "Washington would be willing to talk with Cuba about normalizing relations with no preconditions."[1] This new attitude soon resulted in a bilateral agreement defining fishing rights in overlapping offshore waters, renewal of a bilateral antihijacking agreement, and most significant, the opening of Interest Sections in the nations' respective capitals to conduct diplomatic business.[2] After almost two decades of hostilities, insults, and attacks, the United States and Cuba seemed to have embarked on the road to reconciliation. The U.S. trade embargo against Cuba, its occupation of the Guantanamo naval base, and Cuba's involvement in Africa made the process difficult, but hopes for settling these and other problems were at an all-time high during the Carter administration's first three years.

The new president was not only serious about improving relations with Cuba, he was also determined to change the United States' relationship with most Latin American and other Third World countries, especially those ruled by dictators. When announcing his candidacy in December 1974, Carter committed his administration to high moral and ethical values. He urged that "this country set a standard within the community of nations of courage, compassion, integrity, and dedication to basic human rights and freedoms."[3] Carter had been "deeply troubled" by U.S. policy errors and abuses of power in Vietnam, Cambodia, Chile, and other countries.[4] Thus a new Cuba policy would be in harmony with his new agenda.

Cuba's first reconciliatory signals came in April 1977 from Raúl Castro, Cuban defense minister and vice-president. Speaking to visiting American journalists, Castro said that "the war between the United States and Cuba is over. . . . We are reconstructing the bridges."[5] Those remarks were followed by his brother Fidel's comments to Senator George McGovern during a meeting in Havana. Castro told the senator that "a poor, developing nation had much to gain from commercial relations with the United States; and that once such economic relations had been created, Cuba would have no choice but to consider the value of that relationship as it set its other policies."[6]

Castro's desires for better trade relations with the United States were well known. Since the mid-1970s, he had received a number of trade delegations in Havana to explore the possibilities of ending the embargo. On one occasion he received a standing ovation from fifty-two Minnesota businessmen when he called the trade embargo "a morally unjustified measure of force whose end would make the solution of all problems easier."[7] That Castro was at least willing to talk and perhaps negotiate was in itself considerable progress in comparison to the previous eighteen years. It was up to Carter to decide how far the United States would go to normalize relations with Cuba.

President Carter personally believed that Castro had become disenchanted with the Soviet Union and that a change in Cuban-Soviet relations was perhaps in the making. In his memoirs, the president recalled how during a secret meeting between Castro and National Security Advisor Robert Pastor, the Cuban president had candidly discussed his dissatisfaction with the Soviet Union and his desire for better relations with the United States:

> He described without any equivocation his problems with the Soviet Union; his loss of leadership position in NAM [Nonaligned Nations Movement] because of his subservience to the Soviet Union; his desires to pull out of Ethiopia now, and Angola later; his

involvement in the revolutionary movements in Central America. . . . He is very deeply hurt by our embargo. Wants to move toward better relationships with us, but can't abandon his friends, the Soviets, who have supported his revolution unequivocally.[8]

Whether Castro would continue moving toward better relations with the United States was yet to be seen. Yet Castro was clearly impressed by Carter's style and character. He publicly declared that the new administration, unlike the preceding five, was not characterized by a hostile policy toward Cuba, and that Carter had not committed himself to an aggressive policy against Cuba during the campaign.[9] Castro also described the new president as a man with "a religious ethic, a Christian ethic."[10] Fidel Castro had never referred to an incumbent U.S. president with such praise and respect.

Relations between Cuba and the United States improved steadily through 1977, and so did exile attitudes toward the Cuban revolution. By the mid-1970s a number of groups and individuals, despite risks of terrorist violence, openly advocated peaceful relations with Cuba and an end to the U.S. economic embargo. The Antonio Maceo Brigade, *Areíto*, the Cuban-American Committee for the Normalization of Relations with Cuba, Lourdes Casal, Manuel Espinosa, Casa de las Américas, and the Cuban Resource Center were among the first to raise their voices in favor of a new U.S. Cuba policy under Carter.[11]

The most effective of these groups was the Antonio Maceo Brigade, a group of fifty-five young Cuban exiles who traveled to Cuba in December 1977. During their three-week stay, brigade members worked in a housing construction project and visited schools, factories, places of historical interest, and relatives and friends they had not seen in more than seventeen years.[12]

The Antonio Maceo Brigade's first trip to Cuba was significant in several ways.[13] First, as the *Miami Herald* correctly observed, "It was the largest group of Cuban exiles to come from the United States since the Bay of Pigs invasion."[14] Second, it provided hard evidence that Cuban exiles would be welcome in Cuba if they came in peace.[15] Third, the Cuban government was clearly interested in the project's success and prospects. President Castro, Vice-President Carlos Rafael Rodríguez, and Minister of Culture Armando Hart were among the many top government officials who met with the group.[16] Fourth, it proved that the exile community was not monolithic, that at least a portion of Cuban youths in exile was willing to look at the revolution with an open mind.

The brigade's trip was not well received in Miami and other Cuban communities in the United States. The exile press published numerous articles labeling brigade members "traitors," "Castro agents," "infiltrators," and "Communists." Militant anti-Castro groups also threatened the "traitors" and declared "war against the enemies of Cuba's freedom."[17] In light of the high emotions that characterize exile politics, the strong reactions were not surprising to brigade members, who knew that any direct approach to Castro would certainly attract the hostility of the exile press and militant groups. Besides, as Wayne S. Smith pointed out, the Cuban revolution had always aroused strong emotions, even among non-Cubans:

> In part, these emotions are due to Cuba's geographic proximity. Certainly they are also fueled by the personality of Castro. Many Americans grind their teeth in rage at the sight of him on their TV screens. Congressmen who can discuss in rational terms future relations with Albania or Vietnam angrily exclude that possibility for Cuba. By contrast, a small but equally committed minority idolize Castro as the antiestablishment figure par excellence. Dispassionate analysis between these two extremes is extraordinarily rare.[18]

Smith's observations are accurate. Cuba and Castro are still extremely emotional issues that often sweep away reason and logic. Thus, normalization would take much more than friendly trips by Cuban exiles. Nonetheless, the Antonio Maceo Brigade's trip was a step in the right direction on the long road to better relations, at least between Cuba and the exile community.

The Cuba–Cuban Community Abroad Dialogue

On September 6, 1978, Fidel Castro stunned the Cuban exile community and perhaps the world when he offered the opportunity for a dialogue between his government and exiled Cubans. During a press conference held in Havana and attended by exiled Cuban journalists, as well as by some members of the international press, Castro expressed his willingness to discuss issues of mutual interest to Cuba and the exile community. The proposed agenda would concentrate on family reunification and the release of political prisoners in Cuba, but include other related issues such as family visits to and from Cuba, the permanent return of older exiles and others to Cuba, and exit permits for those who wished to emigrate to the United States.[19]

Most journalists attending the press conference were eager to know why Castro was suddenly interested in a dialogue with the Cuban exiles. Castro explained his decision and the factors that had influenced him:

> There has been a certain change in attitude within the Cuban community abroad and in the opinion of our own people, and the revolution in general as well. I believe that hostility has diminished. Several factors, in fact many factors, have contributed to this. The United States has made some gestures towards Cuba and a certain detente has been brought about between the governments of the United States and Cuba. This has created a particular climate. But there is another essential thing. The Revolution will be twenty years old soon. From our point of view it is absolutely consolidated and irreversible. We know it, the government of the United States knows it too. This is an important factor.[20]

Castro felt confident that a dialogue between Cuba and the "Cuban community abroad" was not only possible but necessary to solve the common problems separating the two communities.[21] He also firmly asserted that the dialogue would include only members of the Cuban community abroad who were in some way representative of the community. The U.S. government would not be invited to the talks.[22]

The exile community's reaction to Castro's invitation was mixed. Almost twenty years of hostility could not be erased overnight. Few could oppose the release of political prisoners, however, some of whom had been in prison for almost two decades. And few could oppose family reunification, when almost every Cuban family in exile remained divided in one way or another. In addition, there were many, especially among the young, who believed the revolution had come of age and that it was time to come to terms with it.

Opposition to the dialogue came mainly from militant anti-Castro groups and their sympathizers. Members of thirty-seven such organizations rejected any kind of dialogue with Castro and called everyone who sought it or participated in it "traitors."[23] Manuel (Tony) de Varona, former prime minister of Cuba under Carlos Prío Socarrás, and long-time exile leader, echoed the "traitor" epithet in reference to dialogue proponents, and added that to talk to Castro would mean to "appease" him.[24] Others such as journalist César J. Torrens were willing to consider a dialogue, but only if the Cuban president first freed all political prisoners, withdrew Cuban troops from Africa, resigned from office, and called for free elections within ninety days. "Maybe then I would return to Cuba, . . . as long as the United States permitted me to take a .30 caliber machinegun with plenty of ammunition, just in case."[25]

The dialogue, like nearly everything Castro had said or done during the previous nineteen years, caused great controversy among the exiles. Still, the humanitarian issues of family reunification and political prisoners' freedom were sufficiently powerful to keep the idea of a dialogue alive, despite vocal and often violent opposition. Dialogue proponents in the United States, Puerto Rico, Venezuela, Spain, and other nations with large Cuban communities organized the Committee-of-75. The Committee, made up of seventy-five prominent exile figures, traveled to Cuba for negotiations with the Cuban government. The group negotiated the lifting of travel restrictions between the United States and Cuba and the release of 3,600 political prisoners from Cuban jails.[26]

Reaction to the negotiations was mixed. Those who participated in them were again labeled "traitors," while a sizable segment of the exile community rejoiced over the talks' success. The humanitarian character of the agreements was simply too strong to be ignored. For example, the *Miami Herald* remained skeptical about Castro's motives but endorsed the dialogue for humanitarian reasons. In an editorial titled "Whatever Castro's Motives, the Prisoners Are Welcome," the paper told its readers:

> The arrival in Miami of the first political prisoners from Cuban jails is a historic occasion in which all persons who love freedom should rejoice. We hope the impetus that made their release possible continues until all political prisoners in Cuba are freed. . . . We add our voice to those who say such dialogue is desirable because it could speed both the release of prisoners and the reunification of Cuban exiles and their families.[27]

The Carter administration also applauded any contact between Cubans in exile and the Castro government that would lead to family reunification and the release of political prisoners.[28]

As the dialogue gained support in Miami and other exile communities, militant anti-Castro groups grew more violent. Violence, however, was not new to those who advocated any kind of peaceful relations with Cuba. From 1973 to 1976, the Federal Bureau of Investigation and local agencies in Miami investigated 103 bombing attempts and six political assassinations.[29] Several years before the dialogue of 1978, Luciano Níeves and Ramón Donéstevez were assassinated in Miami for merely expressing their desires for coexistence with Castro's Cuba.[30]

After the dialogue sessions of November and December 1978, the Committee-of-75 was not the only group in danger of terrorist attacks. Militant anti-Castro organizations extended their threats by "declaring war" against anyone who traveled to Cuba, for any reason. Omega 7, a secret organization of "Cuban partisans combating Fidel Castro's dictatorship and Soviet colonialism,"[31] went on a terror rampage, bombing the Cuban and Soviet missions to the United Nations, travel agencies selling trips to Cuba, an Aeroflot agency, and businesses owned by Committee-of-75 members.[32]

On April 28, 1979, Carlos Muñiz Varela, a member of the Antonio Maceo Brigade and president of Varadero Tours, an agency that organized trips to Cuba for exiles in Puerto Rico, became the first fatality in the anti-dialogue terror campaign when he was shot to death by "Comando Cero" in San Juan, Puerto Rico. Comando Cero used Muñiz Varela's assassination to reiterate its threat to the Committee-of-75 and the community at large: "Any Cuban or Puerto Rican, just as any American who travels to Cuba, regardless of his motives, is considered our enemy. Any Cuban who goes to Cuba, in tourist groups or by himself, we will be forced to judge as we did with Muñiz Varela."[33] Comando Cero also called the Spanish-language radio station WOCN in Miami to warn that Muñiz Varela was "the first to die, but not the last; now there are seventy-four left to execute."[34]

Another victim of the terrorist campaign was Eulalio José Negrín, Committee-of-75 member, assassinated on November 25, 1979. Negrín, like Muñiz Varela, was ambushed by men in passing cars. Only the setting had changed from the streets of San Juan, Puerto Rico, to those of Union City, New Jersey, and Omega 7 claimed the "patriotic" deed this time. It too took the opportunity to publicize the "war" against anyone traveling to Cuba. An anonymous caller told United Press International that Omega 7 would continue with the executions until they "eliminated all traitors living in this country."[35]

The assassinations, bombings, threats, and intimidation continued through 1979, but so did the exiles' trips to Cuba and the prisoner releases. By early 1980, more than 100,000 exiles had visited relatives in Cuba and spent over $100 million there, thus partially alleviating the U.S. trade embargo. The political prisoners program, which included people who had just been released from prison and their families, as well as former prisoners and their families, allowed 22,168 people to emigrate from Cuba to the United States.[36]

The dialogue between the Cuban government and the Cuban community abroad set an important precedent in United States-Cuba relations. By talking and negotiating directly with the exiles, Castro proved that the United States government did not have to be involved in matters affecting the Cuban community in the United States. From January 1979 to March 1980, decisions about which Cubans could travel to and from the United States were approved in Havana first and in Washington later. In general terms, Castro had more control over U.S. immigration policy than Carter.

The Peruvian Embassy Incident

On April 1, 1980, six Cubans in a bus crashed through the gate of the Peruvian embassy in Havana amid a hail of gunfire in which one Cuban guard was killed. The gate crashers solicited and received political asylum from the Peruvian government. Cuba responded by increasing the number of guards and barricades at the embassy gate and demanding that the gate crashers be surrendered to be tried for the death of Pedro Ortiz Cabrera, the Cuban soldier killed during the incident.[37]

The incident at the Peruvian embassy was not isolated or new. For months, Cubans trying to leave the country had been breaking into Latin American embassies in Havana. In March 1980, Peruvian Ambassador Edgardo de Hasbish y Palacio was recalled to Lima after sending away twelve Cubans who had sought asylum in his embassy. Up until the April 1 incident, twenty-five asylum seekers had forced their way into the Peruvian embassy, fifteen into the Venezuelan embassy, and one into the Argentine embassy.[38] The Cuban government did not recognize the political asylum rights of those people, because none of those who entered the embassies through the use of force were involved in political problems, and thus did not need diplomatic asylum.[39]

The Peruvian government refused repeated requests by Cuban authorities to surrender the gate crashers. Cuba then responded by withdrawing all guards and barricades from the embassy compound. In addition, Cuban radio announced that anyone who wanted to leave the country should go to the Peruvian embassy. Neither the Cuban nor Peruvian government was prepared for the spontaneous response to the radio announcement. Within seventy-two hours more than 10,000 people had crowded into the embassy grounds.[40]

The Cuban government explained its position and provided details about the guards' withdrawal on April 4 in a series of articles in *Granma*, believed to have been written by Castro himself. The articles alleged that the vast majority of those who rushed to the embassy after the radio announcements were "scum, criminals, lumpen, parasites, and antisocial elements" and that "none of them were subject to political persecution nor were they in need of the sacred right of diplomatic asylum."[41] Even so, Cuba's policy would be as follows:

1. Cuba is not opposed to having all those who so desire travel legally to Venezuela and Peru as long as they obtain authorization from those countries.
2. Nor does it oppose having them travel to other countries with the authorization of the corresponding government.
3. Those who forced their way into the embassies will not be allowed to leave.
4. Those who entered the Peruvian embassy after the guards were removed are not considered guilty of forced entry and are, therefore, absolutely free to return to their homes and go in and out of the embassy as often as they want. The Cuban authorities will not take measures against them. They can go to Peru or any country which gives them a visa. That is up to them and the country that wants to receive them.[42]

As far as the Cuban government was concerned, the Peruvian embassy affair could be easily solved as soon as Peru or any other country or countries agreed to receive the asylum seekers. To classify all those who wished to leave Cuba as "scum" and "antisocial" was unfair. Cuba's claim, however, that the main motivation for the crowd at the Peruvian embassy was economic and not political was certainly accurate, and would soon be accepted by the U.S. government.

People wanted to leave Cuba for many reasons. Chief among them were: (a) family reunification; when the Cuban airlift was suspended in 1973, tens of thousands were waiting to join their families in the United States and had been unable to do so since; (b) weariness with the sacrifices the revolution required, and desire for a less regimented life in the United States; (c) consumerism, long gone from Cuba's revolutionary austerity, but brought back for a short time during the 1979 dialogue, when Cuban exiles visited the island bringing expensive gifts and success stories about life in the United States; and (d) political dissidence. Many had been disaffected with the government for years and patiently awaited the opportunity to leave.[43]

These explanations did not convince observers and commentators outside Cuba, who almost invariably chose to interpret the events in strictly political terms. The "Havana Ten Thousand," as they came to be known in the U.S. media, were seen by most as a repudiation of Castro and the revolution. Cubans in the United States read the embassy incident as the first signs of "open rebellion" against Castro and the "beginning of the end" for the revolutionary government. Exile communities in Miami, New York City, Union City, and Washington, D.C., staged demonstrations, rallies, and money and food drives in solidarity with the ten thousand at the Peruvian embassy.[44]

In an editorial titled "The Havana Ten Thousand," the *New York Times* interpreted the embassy affair as a "verdict on Castroism" and urged the United States to use it for anti-Castro propaganda in the Caribbean: "In their own way, the only feasible way, the Havana Ten Thousand are rendering a verdict on Castroism. American diplomacy ought to be resourceful to see that this verdict is absorbed throughout the Caribbean, a region searching for new forms of governments."[45] The *Miami Herald* also focused on the repudiation thesis: "Thousands of Cubans, repressed by more than 21 years of Castro's Communist rule and desperate for a chance to live in freedom, went to the embassy."[46]

While the rhetoric of freedom and democracy filled the front pages, the situation inside the Peruvian embassy kept worsening, and Castro personally guaranteed the safety of all those who went home until exit visas could be arranged. To the surprise of those who had interpreted the embassy affair as a statement against Communist repression, Castro's offer was readily accepted by many. About 3,000 people received temporary passes to go home, 747 of whom did not return to the embassy; another 3,187 received permanent passes to stay home and passports and authorization to leave the country.[47]

The unusual arrangement between Castro the "persecutor" and the 10,000 "persecuted" in the embassy prompted some serious reevaluations. The United Nations High Commissioner for Refugees said that the problem was not in his jurisdiction because "scrammers" were not refugees, they were just people wanting to emigrate. *Third World* Magazine journalist Luis Rodríguez dos Santos underlined the contrast between those trying to leave Cuba and those trying to escape right-wing military dictatorships in Latin America: "The thousands of Latin Americans who have had to take to embassies to escape the chamber-of-horrors persecutions of Pinochet, Videla and the Uruguayan generals must have smiled at seeing these 'refugees' leave the embassy at night, to sleep calmly in their homes while awaiting exit documents."[48]

Even William R. Long, managing editor of *El Miami Herald*, argued that while the Havana ten thousand would have gone anywhere, Peru was not exactly where they wanted to go. Most wanted to come to the United States:

> Peru may be free of the Communist yoke, but it's no land of opportunity. It is a miserably poor country, where millions live in squalor and hunger . . . 18 percent of the work force is unemployed, and 47 percent is underemployed . . . 72 of every 1,000 Peruvian babies less than a year old died, compared to 37 per 1,000 in Cuba . . . life is just as hard in Peru, in different but no less vital ways. If they had a chance to get to the United States, 10,000 Peruvians and more would be just as desperate to go as the Havana ten thousand.[49]

It is ironic that Long's article inadvertently repeated Castro's own observations at the time of the Camarioca boatlift fifteen years earlier. Castro claimed then that if the United States extended its open immigration policy toward Cuba to other poor Latin American countries, they would empty out overnight.[50] As far as Castro was concerned, the United States still practiced an open-door immigration policy with regard to Cuba. All he had to do was find a way to set it in motion. No other Latin American government had that option.

Almost a month before the Peruvian embassy incident, in a speech to the Federation of Cuban Women's third congress, Castro raised the possibility of a second Camarioca by publicly criticizing the United States for encouraging illegal departures from Cuba by way of hijacking boats to Florida. The Cuban government felt that while it had responded to U.S. wishes with regard to skyjackings, the United States had not responded to them in kind for maritime hijackings or other illegal departures from Cuba. Castro stated:

> We hope that they [the United States] will adopt measures so they will not encourage the illegal departures from the country because we might also have to take our own measures. We did it once. . . . We were forced to take measures in this regard once. We have also warned them of this. We once had to open the Camarioca port. . . . We feel it is proof of the lack of maturity of the United States Government to again create similar situations.[51]

Castro's public warning was only the latest in a series of indications of his desire to resume normal migration to the United States. In addition, the Cuban government had privately discussed the possibilities of reopening Camarioca months before the embassy incident. Both the Central Intelligence Agency and the State Department were well informed about Cuba's plans as early as January 1980, three months before the embassy incident.[52] The evidence clearly showed that if the opportunity presented itself, Castro would not hesitate to launch another massive migration to the United States.

The rush of more than 10,000 asylum-seeking Cubans into the Peruvian embassy was, if nothing else, an embarrassment to Castro. Castro, however, had turned bad situations for the better in the past and sought to do it again. After all, conditions were generally in his favor: the embassy incident did not represent a serious challenge to his power; he had proven his good faith in negotiations with the Cuban exile community during the dialogue; the U.S. immigration policy toward Cuba had always operated at the crisis level; and precedents for a boatlift and airlift had been established almost fifteen years earlier.

The "Freedom Flotilla"

Napoleón Vilaboa, a Bay of Pigs veteran and Committee-of-75 member, was visiting Cuba at the time of the Peruvian embassy incident. Upon his return to Miami, Vilaboa and a group of fellow exiles decided that perhaps they could persuade the Cuban government to allow them to transport the "Havana ten thousand" to Florida. They organized a flotilla of forty-two privately owned boats and set out for Cuba loaded with medicines and food for the would-be refugees. To their surprise, the Cuban government agreed to open the Port of Mariel, not only to those in the Peruvian embassy but to anyone whose relatives in the states came to Mariel to claim them.[53]

The Cuban government's official announcement of the new boatlift sent shock waves throughout Cuba, Cuban exile communities, and Washington. Just a day before the announcement, April 19, 1980, a massive demonstration of more than a million people marched in front of the Peruvian embassy in Havana to show support for Castro and the revolution. Thousands of Cuban exiles rushed to Key West, Florida, to rent or buy every available vessel and head for Cuba to claim their relatives. In Washington, President Carter pondered the situation with some apprehension but finally reacted with a phrase borrowed from his predecessors: the United States would continue to "provide an open heart and open arms for the tens of thousands of refugees seeking freedom from Communist domination."[54]

Carter's "open heart and open arms" remarks were interpreted as the signal to proceed with the boatlift, and within hours hundreds of boats jammed Mariel Harbor. More than 6,000 Cubans arrived in Key West during the first week of the boatlift, and throughout the month of May, daily arrivals averaged 3,000 persons. The president had inadvertently committed a serious blunder, since his initial reaction to the boatlift had been that it was illegal, and anyone who participated in it would be subject to prosecution. For the moment, confusion ruled and the boatlift continued.

Blame for the confusion should not be assigned wholly to President Carter. After all, Eisenhower and Johnson had reacted the same way to similar Cuban refugee crises during their administrations. Nevertheless, the situation had changed since the Eisenhower and Johnson eras. Under the Refugee Act of March 1980, passed only five weeks before Mariel, the United States had placed a yearly quota of 19,500 refugees from Cuba. In addition, individual case reviews were required before refugee status was granted. The law defined refugees as people who were "unable and unwilling" to return to their homeland because of political, racial, religious, or other persecution.[55] Technically and legally, the Cubans were simply undocumented aliens seeking asylum, not refugees.

The prospect of another massive Cuban migration to Florida alarmed state and federal officials and created a dilemma for them. For months Haitians coming into the state had been denied refugee status (see Chapter 8). If the federal government followed tradition and granted refugee status to the Cubans, it would seemingly have to do the same for the estimated 30,000 illegal Haitians in the state. Refugee status meant that all those eligible would qualify for federal aid. Thus, the status question could mean millions or billions of dollars, depending on the number of Mariel entrants, in state and federal spending. While Florida officials demanded federal action, the administration wavered and the boats kept coming.[56]

In an attempt to stem the tide of Cubans, or at least to make it more orderly, the administration on May 14 made an offer to the Cuban government and reiterated the illegality of the boatlift to those participating in it:

> We are prepared to start an airlift or a sealift immediately as soon as President Castro accepts this offer. Our government is chartering two large, seaworthy ships, which will go to Key West to stand by, ready to go to Cuba. To ensure a legal and orderly process, all people will have to be screened before departure from Cuba. . . . The Coast Guard is now communicating with vessels illegally en route to or from Cuba and those already in Mariel Harbor to tell them to return to the United States without taking Cubans on board. . . . We will do everything possible to stop these illegal trips to Cuba.[57]

The administration's proposal was almost immediately rejected. Boats piloted by Cuban exiles continued bringing "illegals" to Key West by the thousands, risking boat impoundment as well as a thousand-dollar fine per passenger upon arrival. Nearly 9,000

Cubans arrived in Key West in the first two days following the administration's announcement. Castro responded with "the march of the fighting people," in which more than 5 million persons (more than half Cuba's population) participated. There were pro-Cuba support marches in Costa Rica, Peru, Mexico, and Panama.[58]

Fidel Castro was determined to turn the Peruvian embassy incident and subsequent boatlift into a political bonanza for him through demonstrations of support and to embarrass President Carter through defiance. On May Day, before a crowd of one million, and with a number of Latin American heads of state in attendance, Castro defiantly told Carter that Mariel Harbor would remain open: "We are vigorously abiding by our slogan. Anybody who wishes to go to any other country where he is received, good riddance."[59] He had cleverly turned the "escape from communism" line against its principal author. In addition, Castro told the United States that Cuba was willing to talk, not only about refugees but also about the U.S. economic embargo against Cuba, the naval base at Guantanamo, and U.S. spy flights over Cuba.[60] In other words, if the United States wanted an orderly immigration, it would have to discuss other longstanding issues with Cuba. In the meantime, Castro controlled the migration of Cubans to the United States.

Faced with defiance by the Cuban exiles and intransigence from Castro, the federal government was forced to cope with the Cuban influx the way it had in the past. On May 6, President Carter declared a state of emergency in Florida, and a tent city went up in the Orange Bowl Stadium in Miami to accommodate thousands of homeless Cubans. Another tent city was located under Miami's Interstate 95, and tens of thousands of refugees were flown to isolated military bases. Fort Chaffee, Arkansas, Eglin Air Force Base, Florida, Fort Indiantown Gap, Pennsylvania, and Fort Mc-Coy, Wisconsin, became temporary homes for thousands of Cubans waiting to be claimed by family, hoping for sponsors, or detained because of their criminal record in Cuba.[61]

The longer Cubans stayed in the processing centers, the more frustrated they became. They had come to the United States in the "freedom flotilla," but thousands were detained for months, and some were imprisoned for years (see Chapter 7) for crimes committed in Cuba against Castro's government. Confused and frustrated about their plight, the detainees sometimes rioted, demanding their immediate release.[62]

Nightly television news reports and daily newspaper accounts of violent confrontations between the Cubans and the National Guard, the escape of "known criminals" from the camps, and the destruction and burning of federal property by the newly arrived aliens triggered a new wave of resentment and apprehension against the Cuban influx. A Gallup poll revealed that 59 percent of Americans believed the influx of Cubans was bad for the United States, while only 19 percent thought it was good.[63]

By early June 1980, the Mariel boatlift had turned into a major crisis for South Florida and the Carter administration. More than 80,000 Cubans had arrived illegally in Key West, and the end of the boatlift was nowhere in sight. In the meantime, the federal government grappled with the status question: Were the Cubans motivated by economic or political reasons? The Carter administration resisted granting refugee status to the Cubans by arguing that the new arrivals' motivations for leaving Cuba were more economic than political: "In general, their fear of persecution was derived from their own act of leaving Cuba, not necessarily that they had been persecuted by the government before leaving; refugee status would reward illegal entry and set dangerous precedents for future migration; the Cubans were no more deserving of refugee status than the Haitians."[64]

The status question was temporarily settled on June 20 when the administration announced the creation of a new classification: "Cuban-Haitian entrant." Under this classification, the new entrants would be allowed to stay in the United States and could adjust their status to that of "permanent resident alien" after two years. Most important, the entrants would be eligible for medical services, supplemental income, and emergency assistance benefits, and state and local governments would be reimbursed for 75 percent of the program's costs (see Table 6.1).[65]

The Cuban-Haitian classification defused the crisis for the Carter administration but failed to solve the problems associated with a multiple refugee influx (see Chapter 8). In the short run, state and local governments were appeased with reimbursements, and a "dangerous precedent" for future immigrations was avoided. More significant, the new classification broke with the traditional

Table 6.1   1980 Cuban and Haitian Immigration to Dade County After the Federal Census

	Census pop.	Est. num. of refugees Cuban	Haitian	Pop. inc. refugees	% of increase	% Latin	Total % of Latin pop. inc. refugees
Miami	346,865	32,500	12,932	392,297	13.0	56	59
Hialeah	145,254	24,335	581	170,170	17.0	74	78
Miami Beach	96,298	7,950	700	104,948	9.0	22	27
Dade County Total	1,625,781	100,000	21,876	1,747,657	7.5	35	39

Source: Metropolitan Dade County Planning Department, "Cuban and Haitian Refugees: Miami: Standard Metropolitan Statistical Area, 1980," Miami, Florida, January 1981, pp. 14–22. Reprinted with permission from Thomas D. Boswell and James R. Curtis, *The Cuban-American Experience: Culture, Images and Perspectives* (Totowa, N.J.: Rowman & Allanheld, 1984), 81.

special treatment Cubans had received from the Immigration and Naturalization Services.

Before Mariel, Cubans wishing to come to the United States enjoyed a special status in the eyes of immigration officials. That they were coming from Castro's Cuba had been enough to earn them political refugee status, a preference granted to no other Latin Americans:

> The actions of the United States Government in treating the Cubans differently after 1959 led social observers to presume differences in individual motivation. Consequently, "political" roots of migration flows has come to mean those from countries who oppose the United States. Similar political activities in Caribbean countries that support the United States are virtually ignored as producers of "political" refugees. Mariel emerges as a contradiction to this practice. Despite opposition of the United States to the Castro Government, policy towards the latest emigrants has changed considerably.[66]

The Mariel boatlift clearly showed that the United States had no control over immigration from Cuba. From April 20 to September 26, 1980, Cuban immigration to the United States was directed from Havana, not Washington. The Cuban government unilaterally decided when to open and when to close Mariel Harbor for emigration, directed marine traffic to and from Mariel, and decided on each of the 125,000 Cubans who came to the United States during the five months that the operation lasted. In the absence of clearly defined laws to control immigration from Cuba, the Carter administration could classify the Mariel entrants any way it wanted, but it could not stop them. More serious, however, was the president's failure to press the Cuban government to sign a lasting immigration accord. Without it, another boatlift could take place whenever the Cuban government decided to launch it.

Notes

1. *Miami Herald*, February 14, 1977, 14a.
2. Ronald Copeland, "The 1980 Cuban Crisis: Some Observations," *Journal of Refugee Resettlement* 1 (August 1981): 23.
3. Jimmy Carter, *Keeping the Faith: Memoirs of a President* (New York, 1982), 143.
4. Ibid. On May 22, 1977, only five months after his inauguration, Carter officially announced his human rights foreign policy during a speech at Notre Dame University (141–51).
5. *Miami Herald*, April 9, 1977, 1a.
6. *Miami Herald*, April 12, 1977, 19a.
7. *Miami Herald*, April 21, 1977, 32a. The *Miami Herald* also published several articles analyzing the possibilities of trade with Cuba and giving the impressions of business delegations to Cuba. See *Miami Herald*, January 11, 1976, 4, 12a; February 4, 1977, 1a; March 10, 1977,6a; March 28, 1977, 1a; April 3, 1977, 11a. See also Kirby Jones, "Trade Winds A' Changin'," *Cuba Review* 6 (March 1976): 14–18.
8. Carter, *Keeping the Faith*, 479–80.
9. Michael Taber, ed., *Cuba's Internationalist Foreign Policy 1975–1980: Fidel Castro's Speeches* (New York, 1981), 248.
10. Ibid., 261.
11. See Terry Cannon, "U.S Cuban Policy: A Future Stalled in the Past," *Cuba Review* 6 (March 1976): 19–28; "Una iglesia cubana en Miami que apoya el levantamiento del bloqueo a Cuba," *Areíto* 3 (1976): 50–52.
12. For more information on the brigade's activities in Cuba, see *Areíto* 4 (Spring 1978): 1–60; Jesus Díaz, *De la patria y el exilio* (Havana, 1979); *Bohemia*, January 20, 1978, 46–49. Also see the film "Cincuenta y Cinco Hermanos" (Havana, 1978).
13. As of this writing, there have been eight brigade contingents since 1977. The groups vary in size according to the time of travel and length of stay. The largest contingent was the second, with almost 200 members, in the summer of 1979. See *Bohemia*, August 10, 1979, 50–55.
14. *Miami Herald*, February 7, 1978, 3b.
15. To participate in the brigade, members must agree in principal to the following points of unity: (a) favor normalization of relations between the United States and Cuba, (b) favor the lifting of the U.S. economic embargo against Cuba, and (c) call for an end to all hostile acts against Cuba by the U.S. government and members of Cuban exile organization. See *Areíto* 4 (Spring 1978): 4.
16. For more on the brigade's four-hour meeting with Castro, see Luis Rumbaut, "Conversación con Fidel," *Areíto* 4 (Spring 1978): 24–28.

17. *El Expreso,* February 10, 1978; *La Nación,* February 2, 1978; *Réplica,* February 23, 1978; *La Prensa,* February 5, 1978.
18. Wayne S. Smith, "Dateline Havana: Myopic Diplomacy," *Foreign Policy* 48 (Fall 1982): 158–59. Smith was chief of the U.S. interest section in Havana from 1979 to 1982.
19. For more on the press conference, see Fidel Castro, *Entrevista de Fidel con un grupo de periodistas cubanos que escriben para la comunidad cubana en el exterior y varios periodistas norteamericanos* (Havana, 1978); Lourdes Casal, "Fidel Castro: invitación al diálogo," *Areíto* 5 (1978): 5–8; Max Azicri, "Un analisis pragmatico del diálogo entre la Cuba del interior y del exterior," *Areíto* 5 (1979): 4–7.
20. Taber, ed., *Cuba's Internationalist Foreign Policy,* 213; Fidel Castro, *Entrevista,* 11.
21. Castro used the term "Cuban community abroad" for the first time during the September 6, 1978, press conference and explained that he would stop using derogatory terms such as "worms" and "counterrevolutionaries" to describe the exiles. He admitted that those were "unjust generic references to people who had emigrated, unjust generalizations" (Taber, 217).
22. Ibid., 219–20.
23. *Miami Herald,* October 7, 1978, 1b.
24. *Miami Herald,* October 16, 1978, 1b.
25. Quoted in *Miami Herald,* October 7, 1978, 1b.
26. The talks were held in Havana on November 20 and 21 and December 9, 1978. See Taber, *Cuba's Internationalist Foreign Policy,* 221–31. It must be noted that the dialogue did not take place overnight. Secret talks between Castro and a small group of Cuban exiles had been going on for months before the "official" talks took place. An important result of the preliminary talks was the release of fifty political prisoners in October 1978. See *Miami Herald,* October 22, 1978, 33a.
27. *Miami Herald,* October 24, 1978, 6a.
28. *El Miami Herald,* May 3, 1979, 2.
29. *El Miami Herald,* September 22, 1978, 22a.
30. Níeves was assassinated on February 21, 1975, and Donéstevez on April 13, 1976. For more on these two assassinations, see *Miami Herald,* February 22, 1975, and April 14, 1976.
31. Leaflet, Omega 7, "Qué es, quíenes son sus míembros y por que luchan." This is Omega 7's "official" declaration of war/violence against coexistence seekers. They pledged "violence against violence, violence against hypocrisy, and violence for dignity and liberty." The leaflet was published in *La Crónica,* April 30, 1979.
32. For details on these attacks, see Jeff Stein, "An Army in Exile," *New York,* September 10, 1979, 42–49; "Inside Omega 7," *Village Voice,* March 10, 1980, 1, 11–13; and Rubin Herman, "Highest Priority Given by U.S. to Capture of Anti-Castro Group," *New York Times,* March 3, 1980, 1.
33. Press Release, Comando Cero to United Press International offices in San Juan, Puerto Rico, May 20, 1979. Muñiz Varela's assassination received wide press coverage in Miami, New York, and Puerto Rico. See *New York Daily News,* May 21, 1979, 4; *New York Times,* May 1–3, 1979; *Miami Herald,* May 1, 1979, 1b; *Diario de las Américas,* May 4, 1979, 1; *La Crónica,* April 30, 25, and April 31, 1979, 12; Grupo de Investigación Areíto, *Areíto* 5 (1979): 9–11. Also see Luis Adrián Betancourt, *¿Por Qué Carlos?* (Havana, 1981).
34. *El Miami Herald,* May 1, 1979, 2.

35. *Star Ledger* (Union City), November 26, 1979, 1. Negrín's assassination received wide press coverage in New Jersey, New York, and Miami. See *Jersey Journal*, November 27, 1979, 1; *Dispatch* (Union City), November 26, 1979, 1; *New York Times*, November 27, 1979, 1; *Miami Herald*, November 26, 1979, 1, and November 27, 1979, 2; *Guardian*, December 5, 1979, 12.

36. Copeland, "The 1980 Cuban Crisis," 23.

37. *New York Times*, April 6, 1980, 4.

38. Ibid.

39. *Granma*, April 4, 1980, 2.

40. The quick and sizable response to Castro's offer made headlines throughout Cuba and the United States. See *Granma*, April 7, 1980, 1; *Bohemia*, April 12, 1980, 4–8; *New York Times*, April 7, 1980, 1; *Miami Herald*, April 7, 1980, 1a; *Washington Post*, April 7, 1980, 1.

41. Luis Rodríguez dos Santos, "The Emigrants," *Third World* 5 (1980): 18.

42. *Granma*, April 7, 1980, 2.

43. Lourdes Casal, "Cuba, Abríl–Mayo 1980. La historia y la histéria," *Areíto* (1980): 15–25; Peter Winn, "Is the Cuban Revolution in Trouble?" *Nation*, June 7, 1980, 682–85.

44. For more on the exiles' demonstrations, including pictures, see *El Miami Herald*, April 8, 1980, 1; April 12, 1980, 44; April 15, 1980, 13; *Miami Herald*, April 17, 1980, 7a.

45. *New York Times*, April 9, 1980, 26a.

46. *Miami Herald*, April 8, 1980, 6a.

47. *Granma*, April 14, 1980, 2.

48. Rodríguez dos Santos, "The Emigrants," *Third World* 5 (1980): 20.

49. William R. Long, "Peru Is No Bargain, Either," *Miami Herald*, April 27, 1980, 3n. It is interesting to note that a similar article appeared in *Bohemia*. See Reinaldo Peñalver, "El Peru que no conocen los asilados," *Bohemia*, April 25, 1980, 79–81.

50. Lockwood, *Castro's Cuba*, 291.

51. Staff Report, U.S. House of Representatives, Subcommittee on Oversight, Permanent Select Committee on Intelligence, "The Cuban Emigres: Was There a U.S. Intelligence Failure?" June 1980 (Washington, D.C.), 3. For the full text of Castro's speech, see "No sería posible escribír la historia de nuestra Revolución en los ultimos 20 años sin la Federación de Mujeres Cubanas," *Bohemia*, March 14, 1980, 50–61.

52. U.S. House of Representatives, "The Cuban Emigres," 2–3.

53. *Newsweek*, May 5, 1980, 59. Before Vilaboa's action, the Cuban government had canceled flights from Havana to San José, Costa Rica, claiming that the flights were being used for propaganda against Cuba, and that the asylees would have to go directly to their permanent destinations, mainly the United States. For more details on Costa Rica's role in the negotiations and the massive demonstrations held in Havana on April 19, 1980, see *Jamás nos rendiremos* (Havana, 1980).

54. Quoted in Copeland, "The Cuban Crisis," 26. Like the Camarioca boatlift of 1965, news of Mariel's opening made headlines throughout Cuba and the United States. Again, the most reliable source for day-to-day details about the operation was the mass media in both Cuba and the United States. See *Miami Herald*, *New York Times*, *Granma*, and *Bohemia* for the period of April 20 to September 27, 1980.

55. Coordinating Council of Dade County, "Light the Lamp," (Miami, 1980), 11–13.

56. *Miami Herald* took the lead in calling for federal action. For a sample of

the paper's editorial stand on federal aid, see "U.S. Policy Invited Refugees, So U.S. Must Pay the Freight," *Miami Herald*, May 15, 1980, 6a; "Carter Cavils While Refugees Burn," *Miami Herald*, June 3, 1980, 6a; "Cuban Influx Forces Dade to Seek Flood Protection," *Miami Herald*, June 4, 1980, 6a; and "Refugee Agony Needs More Than a Tent City Solution," *Miami Herald*, July 26, 1980, 6a.

57. For the full text of the White House statement, see *Miami Herald*, May 15, 1980, 18a. For more on Carter's attempts to stop the sealift, and the Cuban exiles' response to them, see Mario A. Rivera, "Refugee Chess: Policy by Default," *Caribbean Review* 13 (Fall 1984): 4–6, 36–39.

58. For more on the demonstrations, see *Respuesta del pueblo combatiente* (Havana, 1980; *La primera batalla de toda una generación de jóvenes* (Havana, 1980); Lourdes Casal, "Cuba, Abríl-Mayo," *Areíto* 6 (1980): 15–25; Geoffrey Fox, "The Cuban Exodus and the U.S. Press," *Cuba Update* 1: 4–10.

59. *Miami Herald*, May 2, 1980, 30a.

60. For the full text of Castro's speech and the views of other Latin American leaders who spoke at the rally, see "Con el pueblo no se juega," *Bohemia*, May 9, 1980, 50–64; *Una batalla por nuestra soberanía* (Havana, 1980); and *Granma*, May 11, 1980, 1–6.

61. Fox, "The Cuban Exodus," *Cuba Update*, 7.

62. Rioting and protests took place in all five detention centers. For more on what led to the riots and their consequences, see Paul Heath Hoeffel, "Fort Chaffee's Unwanted Cubans," *New York Times Magazine*, December 21, 1980, 30–31, 42, 44, 47, 50, 52; Nick Nichols, "Castro's Revenge," *The Washington Monthly*, March 1982, 39–42; *Miami Herald*, June 3, 1980, 6a; August 10, 1980, 29a, and August 17, 1980, 1a.

63. *Newsweek*, May 26, 1980, 25.

64. Copeland, "The Cuban Crisis of 1980," 30.

65. Ibid.

66. Robert L. Bach, "The New Cuban Exodus: Political and Economic Motivations," *Caribbean Review* 11 (Winter 1982): 23.

7

Mariel: Aftermath and Consequences

> We consider these refugees [Cubans who went to Peru] as
> seekers of visas [to the U.S.] in a traditional sense since they
> have already found asylum here [Peru] that means that they
> have to try and get a visa just like any other person applying,
> including thousands of Peruvians.
>
> U.S. Consular Official, Lima, Peru November 1983

Searching for Answers

THE MARIEL BOATLIFT was the subject of innumerable
press articles and stories of heroism, determination, suffering,
disillusionment, and hope. Many of the more than 125,000 Cubans
who made the perilous crossing from Mariel to Key West provided
fascinating stories about the Peruvian embassy incident, life in
Cuba, and the social dynamics leading to the exodus that were
reported widely by the press.[1]

Such extensive reporting not only dramatized the refugees'
plight, but it also placed the exodus in a political framework that
was at times far removed from reality. According to most early
press accounts, something seemed to be wrong with the Cuban
revolution, and both its detractors and supporters searched to find
out what:

> For those in this country who have always viewed the Cuban
> Revolution with hostility, the embarrassing mass exodus to the
> United States only confirms their views of it as a totalitarian dicta-
> torship enclosing a captive people who would take the first freedom
> flight available to this land of liberty. For those who have viewed
> the Cuban Revolution with greater sympathy, the stream of head-

lines, images and refugees coming out of Cuba is at best confusing and at worst disillusioning.[2]

Initially, it was not easy to determine the real causes of the exodus, and confusion reigned for at least two months. Then many in the press, the Carter administration, and the public at large realized that perhaps Castro was right all along when he said that most people leaving Cuba did so for economic, not political, reasons. That being the case, Mariel differed from other Latin American migrations in method but not in motive:

> The most striking thing about the new wave of Cuban exiles arriving in Key West is that so few of them are political refugees, despite efforts in Miami to paint them in those colors. Although some cite political or religious reasons for their migration, most stress personal economic goals as their motivation for the boat trip from Mariel. Caribbean and Latin American migrants in search of economic opportunities are nothing new in the United States. On the contrary, significant portions of the populations of Haiti and Mexico, Puerto Rico and the Dominican Republic have made the journey North—one-fifth of the Caribbean's inhabitants came to our shores since World War II alone.[3]

During the boatlift's final weeks, the press began focusing on the new reality the most recent exodus had brought Miami and the federal government: what to do about some 60,000 Cubans without relatives or friends in the United States. Many had come not to escape political persecution or to reunite with their families, but simply to try their luck in the "land of opportunity" or because, as was often said, Castro had sent them to "clean out" Cuba and to make trouble in the United States. For whatever reason, they had arrived to stay and the U.S. government would have to find a solution to the problem.

Many in Miami were outraged at the "tent city" solution the federal government chose for the homeless Cubans. The *Miami Herald* became one of the leading voices calling for more federal aid for refugee relief and a coherent U.S. immigration policy:

> Every Miamian and every American should be ashamed of the continuing presence of the tent city that squats in the shadow of the stately old Dade County courthouse downtown. Federal funds and Miami City employees are maintaining an unprecedented and utterly unacceptable urban slum in the heart of the city. It must go, and quickly. . . . They are an affront to the conscience of the

community and an indictment of the nation's sense of humanity.
. . . There should be a permanent Federal program to relocate
Caribbean entrants to parts of the country where housing and jobs
are available. And long range, the Government will have to develop
a coherent and enforceable immigration policy.[4]

In addition to the eight hundred refugees living in the tent city,
thousands of suspected or admitted criminals awaited resettlement
in the processing centers. According to Nick Nichols, deputy
assistant director for public affairs for the Cuban-Haitian Task
Force, the administration's main reasons for establishing the processing centers were evidently contradictory: "The centers allowed
the government to do a better job of identifying dangerous refugees and isolating them from the community. The second purpose
was to encourage private citizens to sponsor the Cubans, thereby
taking them off the government's hands."[5] It is no wonder that few
jumped at the opportunity to sponsor people whom the federal
government identified as "dangerous."

While thousands hopefully awaited sponsors, the exodus began
to lose its luster in the public eye. The stories of heroism, defiance,
and will power were quickly replaced by "Marielito" horror stories.
The label "Marielito" stigmatized all who came to the United
States during the Mariel boatlift by implying that they were either
criminals or social misfits. *U.S. News and World Report* described
them as "representatives of the most despised immigration in this
nation's history. They came—125,000 of them all at once—in the
boatlift from Mariel, Cuba, with tattered clothes and soiled repu-
tations."[6]

In Miami, "Marielitos" were blamed for increased rates of
murder and rape in 1980. Undoubtedly some Mariel entrants were
responsible for murders and rapes, but as Monsignor Bryan
O'Walsh suggested, data on which the charges were based were far
from clear:

It is true that the Jackson Memorial Hospital Rape Center reports
a doubling of Hispanics being identified as the aggressor by victims
in the months following Mariel. Increases were noted also in the
Black-American and white-American categories. For October
[1980], the figure for Hispanic aggressors was 13 compared with 17
last January [before Mariel]. . . . Meanwhile, the Mariel refugees
are a convenient scapegoat, the only one that can provide the
excuse for getting more federal dollars. All I ask is that the authori-

ties provide the community with factual information and not estimates that tend to further polarize this already divided community.[7]

Monsignor Walsh was not the only community leader calling for
a more objective and rational analysis of the Mariel refugees. His
feelings were echoed by many and opposed by an equal number.
Thus, the debate, fueled by a barrage of letters to the editor, guest
columns, and editorials, raged for months in the Miami papers.
The debate illustrated an unfortunate but emerging polarization
between pre-Mariel and Mariel exiles. Pre-Mariel exiles feared
that their hard-earned reputation as successful migrants would be
tarnished by the "Marielito" stigma. The new refugees, on the
other hand, resentfully rejected the arbitrary label, and many
joined the verbal debate, attempting to prove that they were as
honest, hard-working, and professionally qualified as those who
had left Cuba twenty years earlier.[8]

Mariel entrants not only resented their stigmatization, but also
felt betrayed by family members and friends who had deliberately
lied to them with tales about gold-paved streets, easy millions, fast
cars, and big yachts that lured many of them into coming to the
United States. Roberto Ramírez is a good example of such tragic
folly.

In 1959 Ramírez was a fifteen-year-old student who, like most
young men of his generation, was "at least excited" by the revolution. His father, who was bitterly opposed to Castro and the
revolution, sought to leave the country as quickly as possible. Thus
Roberto was prohibited from becoming "integrated" into the revolutionary process and was forced to lead a double life: pro-revolu-
tion in public and anti-revolution at home. The practice of duplicity
and his sense of being torn between two worlds had a profound
effect on the youth's development.

Ramírez's father kept putting off the family's departure until he
was "simply too old to emigrate," but he never gave up the idea of
Roberto becoming a good anti-Communist. Roberto never joined
the Cuban Communist party, but he was able to get along in the
socialist society. He became a technician and eventually the manager of a large pharmaceutical products plant in Havana, got
married, had two children, saved money, and had many friends.
He led a perfectly normal life until 1979, when an old friend who
had been living in Miami since 1961 came to visit and assured

Roberto that in the United States he could become a millionaire in just a few years.

Taking his friend's advice, Roberto Ramírez left family, work, and friends and came to the United States in the Mariel boatlift to look for the easy fortune he was promised. Today Ramírez is a bitterly disheartened man living in poverty, without a family and with few friends. He describes the past five years as a "nightmare of frustrations in a country where my own people have not only turned their backs on me, but ruthlessly exploited my work and even cheated me of the only thing I own: my skills. . . . I regret ever coming to this country and would go back to Cuba in a minute, but that is impossible and I must pay for my mistakes."[9]

Roberto Ramírez's story is not unique. There were hundreds, perhaps thousands of cases like his, including hundreds who were returned to the tent cities or to the resettlement camps days or weeks after their arrival because their families could not support them and could not deliver on the "fortunes." A survey conducted among the refugees revealed that 80 percent were unemployed three months after their arrival.[10] They too felt betrayed, and some were not willing to accept their fate. During August 1980, six U.S. commercial flights were hijacked to Cuba by Mariel refugees trying to return home, and the federal government had to place armed sky marshals on random flights to stop the disaffected Marielitos.[11]

The hijacking issue was an old point of contention between the Cuban and U.S. governments. The two governments had signed an antihijacking agreement in 1973, but the Cubans unilaterally renounced the agreement in 1976 in retaliation for the blowing up of a Cuban airliner off the coast of Barbados by Cuban exile terrorist Orlando Bosch. Cuba called the act a CIA plot.[12] Although Cuban authorities arrested returning Mariel refugees, and rapidly returned the aircraft and passengers, they refused to send back the hijackers to be tried in U.S. courts, claiming that the U.S. government was responsible for the hijackings. A *Miami Herald* editorial reminded Americans that the hijackings were largely a by-product of the United States' incoherent Cuba policy:

> Americans should remember that the 1980 cycle of hijackings didn't begin with Cuban refugees commandeering airliners from Miami in August. Rather, it began in January when 67 Cubans seized a dredge barge to come to Florida. Since then, four other vessels have been hijacked to the United States, a fact that the

Cuban government resents deeply. . . . Until this month, those Cuba-to-Florida hijackers were not prosecuted by American authorities. The U.S. Government needs a coherent policy on Cuba and Cubans. On hijacking, for example, Americans logically cannot condone a crime of violence when its perpetrator is headed North, but condemn it when the criminal wants to go South.[13]

Hijackings from the United States to Cuba subsided by late 1980, but in May 1983 another rash of sky heists prompted the Federal Aviation Administration to order plain clothes marshals again on commercial aircrafts.[14]

The hijackings, coupled with Miami's rising crime rates and the refugees' high unemployment rate, enhanced the Marielitos' stereotyped image as vagrant or criminal. Nonetheless, statistics show that, contrary to that negative image, Mariel refugees resembled Cubans who had earlier come to the United States. Like the earlier migrants, almost all Mariel refugees had relatives in the United States, and 40 percent were reunited upon arrival. Most had at least an eighth grade education and a history of fairly steady employment in Cuba. As sociologist Robert Bach concluded, most Mariel refugees were neither marginal nor deviant.[15]

Siro del Castillo, associate director of the Department of Human Resources at Fort Chaffee, raised his voice against the unjust labels applied to the Mariel entrants long before researchers got around to interpreting their statistical studies. In a passionate guest column published in *El Miami Herald*, del Castillo reminded the pre-Mariel Cuban community that they were not without sin. "During the past twenty years, many Cubans have made front-page news for their crimes, drug business, embezzlement, illegal gambling, and tax evasion. . . . The list goes on." He also reminded the community that responsibility for the refugees' arrival in the United States lay ultimately with the exile Cubans for bringing them. According to del Castillo, the best and most humane solution to the refugee situation would be for the established Cuban community to do more to help these brothers and sisters. After all, "if we don't help them survive and succeed, their failure will not be theirs alone, but also ours."[16]

Those Who Went to Peru

On August 30, 1980, more than 150 Cuban refugees stormed into Lima's international airport, broke through a plate glass window in a lounge and, ducking bullets fired by airport security guards, proceeded to take fifteen hostages in a Braniff International DC-8 jet. The refugees were part of a group of 740 Cubans who had arrived in Peru from Havana in April. They demanded to be flown to Miami and resettled in the United States. [17]

Almost twenty-four hours later, the refugees peacefully surrendered their hostages and themselves to Peruvian authorities after the U.S. State Department ruled that they were not eligible for admission to the United States as refugees because they had already been resettled in Peru. The State Department's decision was based on the fact that the Cubans, who fled their homeland allegedly to escape communism and totalitarianism, had found a home in a country with a capitalist economy and democratic government. Thus they were no longer in danger of persecution.

Since their arrival in Peru, the Cubans had been living in a tent city in Túpac Amaru Park in Lima. They saw Peru as just a stopover before final resettlement in the United States. After all, they, by risking arrest in the Peruvian embassy in Havana, were largely responsible for the boatlift that took 125,000 Cubans to the United States. The irony of their situation was not lost on analysts and policy makers as they set out to explain the Mariel boatlift and its aftermath to different constituencies.

When asked to explain why, after twenty-one years of revolution, hundreds of thousands wanted to leave the country, Carlos Rafael Rodríguez, vice-president of the Politbureau of the Cuban Communist Party and vice-president of the Council of State, responded:

> Our underdevelopment still promotes problems such as people without the necessary level of consciousness to understand and to practice their social obligations; people who prefer to obtain their income from small illicit businesses, from gambling, from theft. It would be utopian to think that a young socialism with severe economic obstacles to overcome, like ours, would be free of such problems. It is important to point out that, as has been proven, most of these antisocial sectors do not just want to "leave Cuba," they don't want to go to Peru or Colombia; they want to go to the U.S. They look for a way of manifesting, in the turbulent American society, those characteristics which Cuban society, in the process of building socialism, totally rejects. [18]

The Cuban press and media focused attention on the refugees' plight and their disappointment with the United States and living conditions in Peru. A television documentary, "Cubanos en el Peru: Dos Años Despues" (Cubans in Peru: Two Years Later), was particularly telling. The half-hour show described living conditions in Túpac Amaru Park as "terrible" and the refugees as "victims of a mirage and imperialist propaganda." Several interviews with the refugees focused on their amazement with Peru's "strange democracy" where millions lived marginal lives in abject poverty.

The documentary's main focus, however, was on the refugees' complaints and disenchantment with their "new life." They complained about racial discrimination, unemployment, high prices and low salaries, the government's broken promise to help them, and the "terrible" food served in the camps. Viewers were reminded that just a few blocks from the tent city, Peruvians lived in even worse conditions than the Cubans. In shanty towns paradoxically called "pueblos jóvenes," hundreds of thousands lived in wood and cardboard shacks without electricity, running water, sewage systems, or government aid.[19]

A year after the documentary's airing on Cuban television, Roberto Fabricio, *El Miami Herald*'s editor, surprised the Miami-Cuban community with his report on the Cubans of Túpac Amaru Park. Fabricio's article, commentaries, and observations were strikingly similar to those made by the Cuban government's media. Explaining the refugees' complaints about the food, Fabricio wrote: "The food is hardly gourmet fare. But a quick tour of Lima and its 'pueblos jóvenes'—the slums that house hundreds of thousands in substandard living conditions—shows that the food there is no better and no worse. The refugees are getting about what the masses of Peruvians eat."[20]

Legally excluded from the United States, the disgruntled Cubans had only two options: to remain in Peru where they had already been granted political asylum, or to go to other countries that would take them. With help from international refugee aid organizations, many decided on the second option, and in 1980, 225 went to Canada. The following year, 35 went to Brazil, and in 1982, 15 went to Australia.[21] Yet, more than four years after their arrival in Peru, more than 300 Cubans still living in Túpac Amaru Park refused to leave the premises until they were allowed to go to the United States.

When the Peruvian government evicted the group from the park, one-third accepted United Nations' free housing, another third settled somewhere else in Lima, and the rest staged a protest across the street from the United Nations' Lima office.[22] They feared that once the park camp was dismantled, the world would forget their plight and their hopes of going to the United States would be gone forever. Antonio Varona, a Cuban exile leader in Miami who organized relief efforts for the Cubans in Peru, accurately summarized their feelings: "They are dead set on coming to the United States. You could offer them a palace in Lima and they would still turn it down."[23]

As of this writing, several hundred Cubans in Peru, Panama, and Costa Rica still would do anything necessary to emigrate to the United States. They were the real heroes of the Peruvian Embassy. In April of 1980, they paved the way for 125,000 Cubans to emigrate to the United States but were denied that opportunity themselves. Such is the bitter irony of those who went to Peru.

The "Excludables-Undesirables" Dilemma

While the Cubans in Peru complained about their living conditions and the irony of their fate, a group of 1,050 "excludables" or "undesirables" were detained indefinitely at the maximum-security federal penitentiary in Atlanta, Georgia. The federal government classified as "excludable aliens" people whose mental or criminal past rendered them ineligible for release into the general population. They could not be released from jail because they were deemed "unfit for American society."[24] Under immigration law they were not recognized as having entered the country, yet they were in prison here and were not entitled to the legal counsel and other constitutional rights afforded American prisoners.

Allegations, rumors, and stories about Castro's plan to rid himself of Cuba's "anti-socials," "scum," and "crazies" had been making headlines since the "freedom flotilla's" first days.[25] Castro himself was among the first to use derogatory terms to describe the emigrants, and, although he denied using the boatlift to send criminals and mental patients to the United States, it was evident that the Cuban government accepted homosexuality, prostitution, and criminality in general as reasons for emigrating. All anyone wishing to emigrate had to do was admit, without proof, "deviant" or "antirevolutionary" behavior and permission would likely be granted.[26] Thus many lied about their personal integrity to obtain exit permits.

For those who were in prison at the time of the boatlift, the Cuban government's emigration procedures were even more liberal. Except for a select group of political cases, prisoners wishing to go to the United States were released immediately and transported to Mariel to await passage to Key West.

Raúl Quevedo's case was not uncommon. He was serving the third year of a seven-year term for stealing supplies from an army warehouse. At the time of the boatlift, Quevedo was approached by prison officials who offered him the option of immediate emigration to the United States. Quevedo recalls that he, like many of his fellow immates, was suspicious at first, thinking that the offer could be a "trick." Eventually he took the offer. He is convinced, however, that suspicion led hundreds to decline the offer.[27]

Quevedo, like many other prisoners who opted for emigration, was under the impression that "if you had committed a crime in Cuba, you were welcomed as a hero in the United States." Upon his arrival in Key West, Quevedo "proudly" admitted his crime and expected preferential treatment. After all, he had been "treated like a hero" by the boat's captain and most of the sixty passengers on board. "I was shocked when the cop [Immigration and Naturalization Service agent] responded to my tales of crimes against Castro by giving me a ticket to hell, Fort Chaffee, where I spent the most confusing and miserable eight months of my life."[28]

Except for occasional *Miami Herald* editorials and letters to the editors by the inmates themselves, the plight of the 1,050 Cubans in the Atlanta prison went largely unnoticed until July 7, 1983, when U.S. District Judge Marvin Shoob ruled that the United States could not hold illegal aliens indefinitely without giving them some of the constitutional rights of all U.S. citizens.[29] The judge ordered the Immigration and Naturalization Service to begin new hearings for each of the Cuban detainees within sixty days. He also said that a "neutral decision-maker" would have to preside at the hearings, meaning that the Immigration and Naturalization Service could no longer serve as judge and jury to decide whether the Mariel Cubans could be paroled or not.[30] The government would have to prove, case by case, that each jailed Cuban was criminally dangerous to justify his continued detention for society's protection.

Shoob's decision provoked mixed reactions. On the positive side, civil libertarians hailed it as a landmark decision that for the first time granted limited constitutional rights to illegal aliens. On the negative side, the Justice Department responded by appealing the decision on the grounds that the Cubans "have admitted to committing, in Cuba, over fifty murders, over twenty rapes, over thirty arsons, over six hundred robberies and thefts and numerous other crimes."[31] President Reagan supported the appeal for "national security" reasons. He believed that the Cuban government had infiltrated subversive agents into the United States under the guise of refugees fleeing the island.[32] The Cuban community in Miami also reacted negatively. A poll commissioned by the Cuban-American National Foundation, an anti-Castro lobbying group, revealed that 77.3 percent of the 520 Dade County residents of Cuban origin polled opposed the prisoners' release.[33]

Most opponents of the Shoob decision wanted the undesirables deported to Cuba, a proposition the Cuban government consistently rejected throughout 1983. Finally, on December 14, 1984, Ricardo Alarcón Quesada, Cuban deputy minister of foreign affairs, and Michael G. Kozak, deputy legal adviser of the State Department, met in New York City to sign a pact that would allow the return of "undesirables" to Cuba and reopen normal immigration to the United States.[34]

Under the agreement, which was the first U.S. accord with Cuba since Ronald Reagan's election in 1980, Cuba would take back 2,746 mental patients and criminals who came to the United States during the Mariel boatlift. The United States would issue visas, in 1985, to 3,000 political prisoners and their families, and to as many as 20,000 other Cubans. In following years, visas would be issued at the rate of 20,000 annually.[35]

The agreement would allow the United States to return not only excludables who had committed crimes in Cuba before arriving in the United States, but also refugees who had committed crimes in the United States. The main obstacle in the deportation process was a second Judge Shoob decision on October 15, 1984. That ruling stipulated that the refugees officially classified as excludables were entitled to hearings on their claims to political asylum in the United States. Shoob ordered the Board of Immigration Appeals to hold a hearing to decide whether the excludables were entitled to asylum.[36]

Judge Shoob's determination to protect the excludables' rights to due process would probably slow the deportation process and even prevent the deportation of some, but in general, the immigration pact between the United States and Cuba was viewed as an important positive beginning. The *Miami Herald* called it a commendable first step and hoped for other actions to normalize migration between the United States and Cuba and other areas of mutual concern:

> When the new Congress convenes in January 1985, one of its first priorities should be to repeal the Cuban Adjustment Act of 1966. Now that they may migrate legally to the United States, Cubans no longer need the preferential migratory status that they've enjoyed for the past 18 years. . . . A second step might include negotiations over radio jamming from Cuba and cooperation on drug interdiction and search and rescue missions at sea. A third step would require only that Cuba agree to take back more than 1,000 homesick Mariel entrants who want to go back. That would complete the cycle. Migration between Cuba and the United States then would be truly normal. The pact then could be welcomed heartily.[37]

The *Herald*'s expectations began materializing on February 21, 1985, when the first Mariel excludables were deported to Cuba. In accordance with Judge Shoob's ruling, the group of twenty-three were found ineligible for political asylum and flown to Cuba along with legal documents pertaining to their cases.[38] Immigration and Naturalization Service Commissioner Alan C. Nelson hailed the event as "a very proud day for all Americans with the success of this agreement and the actual return of this group."[39] In Havana, the deportees were received by immigration officials and referred to as "a group of twenty-three Cuban citizens" returning in keeping with the "normalization of migratory procedures" between the United States and Cuba.[40]

Unexpectedly, the deportation of Mariel excludables marked the beginning of a new chapter in U.S. immigration history. For the first time since 1945, the United States agreed to return people to a Communist country, a fact all the more remarkable in the context of U.S.–Cuban relations since 1959.

Battle of the Airwaves

The auspicious and hopeful beginnings of the immigration agreement between Cuba and the United States were abruptly shattered at 5:30 A.M. on May 20, 1985, by the words "Buenos días Cuba. Este es Radio Martí." The Reagan administration-sponsored radio broadcasts from the Voice of the Americas studios in Washington, D.C., were aimed at telling the Cuban people the ostensible truth about Fidel Castro and the Cuban government. Its announced purpose: "the right of all men to be free, to obtain information, to find its truth and display it among men who respect it."[41]

Cuba's response to the broadcasts was quick, angry, and retaliatory. In a note dated May 19, 1985, delivered to the United States Interest Section in Havana, the Cuban government denounced Radio Martí as subversive, insulting, and detrimental to future U.S.–Cuba relations:

> As a result of the cynical and provocative decision of the Government of the United States to start subversive broadcasts against Cuba as of May 20, a grim and shameful date which recalls the military occupation of Cuba by the United States, the plunder of its best lands and other natural resources, the neocolonization of our country, and the pseudo-republic accompanied by an amendment to its constitution which gave the United States the right to intervene in Cuba, to which must be added the gross insult of raising the glorious name of José Martí for these broadcasts, deeply wounding the feelings of the Cuban people.[42]

The Cuban government decided to take the following actions:

First, to suspend all proceedings related to the implementation of the agreement on migratory questions signed between the delegation of the two governments on December 14, 1984, in the City of New York.

Second, to suspend all trips by citizens of Cuban origin living in the United States to Cuba, except for those authorized on strictly humanitarian grounds.

Third, the government of Cuba plans to adopt additional measures regarding communications between the United States and Cuba.

Fourth, the government of Cuba reserves the right to reconsider the cooperation it has been unilaterally providing to the government of the United States in the struggle against illegal exits from the country and other activities in which the United States benefits from the spontaneous and selfless cooperation of Cuba.

Fifth, the government of Cuba reserves the right to transmit medium wave radio bradcasts to the United States to make fully known the Cuban view on the problems concerning the United States and its international policy.[43]

Cuba's cancellation of the migration agreement affected thousands in Cuba and the United States. Most immediately affected, however, were the remaining 2,545 excludables scheduled for deportation during the next two years. Without the agreement, the Immigration and Naturalization Service had to stop deportations, placing the excludables in a legal limbo. A similar uncertainty confronted the 3,000 former political prisoners waiting to emigrate to the United States under the agreement. When Radio Martí went on the air, only 201 excludables had been deported to Cuba and only eleven former political prisoners admitted to the United States.[44]

Radio Martí was not a new idea. The project had been in the making for more than four years and enjoyed solid support from President Reagan and noted conservative senators such as Paula Hawkins, Lawton Chiles, Jessie Helms, John Glenn, and Jeremiah Denton. Government-sponsored anti-Castro broadcasts to Cuba were not new either. In March 1960, only fifteen months after Castro's triumph, the Voice of America resumed Spanish-language broadcasts "edited with an eye toward Cuba." In April 1960, Congress authorized the United States Information Agency to use $100,000 for a short-term increase in Spanish-language broadcasts "to cultivate friendship with the people of Cuba and to offset anti-American broadcasts in that country."[45]

Voice of America programs and regular A.M. radio frequencies from Miami stations had been accessible to Cubans for generations, and the Cuban government did little to jam them or keep people from listening to them.[46] Yet, Thomas O. Enders, assistant secretary for inter-American affairs, justified Radio Martí on the grounds that "for twenty-four years, [Cubans] have been denied the basic tools of modern civilized society on which to make judgments—the free flow of information."[47]

To demonstrate the administration's serious commitment to Radio Martí, Enders further defended the broadcasts by citing moral and humanitarian ideals stated in the U.S. Constitution and by quoting Article Nineteen of the United Nations' Universal Declaration of Human Rights: "Everyone has the right to freedom of opinion and expression; this right includes freedom to hold opinions without interference and to seek, receive and impart information and ideas through any media and regardless of frontiers."[48] These were hypocritical words from an administration that recently had prohibited U.S. citizens from receiving newspapers and magazines from Cuba.[49]

The Reagan administration's intransigence on Radio Martí and the Cuban government's equally hard-headed response were politically inopportune and unwise, because for the first time in more than twenty-five years, the United States and Cuba had agreed on procedures that would normalize the chronically abnormal migration between the two countries. The agreement signed in December 1984 would have benefited both governments, as well as the Cuban people in both Cuba and the United States. Cuba would rid itself of disaffected citizens, allowing the revolution to proceed with the participation of a generally sympathtic populace. The United States would admit only 20,000 Cubans for permanent residency each year, thus replacing the chaotic Camarioca and Mariel experiences with a manageable immigration process. Finally, Cuban families divided for twenty-five years would continue the process of reunification.

The only immediate beneficiaries from Radio Martí were the Cuban exile anti-Castro activists who believed that the broadcasts would be detrimental to Castro. In the short run, Radio Martí was a victory for groups like the Cuban-American National Foundation, a research organization dedicated, according to its chairman Jorge Más Canosa, to "providing the right information to the right people in Washington." With that aim, the foundation launched a successful lobbying campaign that proved the Cuban community's political skills and clout at the national level. In addition to informing sympathetic legislators about Cuba, the foundation contributed hundreds of thousands of dollars to their campaigns.[50]

The foundation's generosity with legislators sympathetic to its cause was recognized by Reagan himself during an official visit hosted by the group to Miami's Little Havana. During his speech to a selected audience of prominent Cuban exiles, the president remarked: "The greatest threat to dictators like Fidel Castro is the truth. That is why I am urging the Congress to approve legislation for the establishment of Radio Martí." His comment was received with thunderous applause, and it refurbished illusions of Castro's impending demise.[51]

Reagan made good on his promise to the Cuban exiles. Radio Martí's $10 million budget was approved shortly after the president's visit to Miami, and the broadcasts began exactly two years later. Radio Martí's budget, however, was only part of the price the United States would have to pay, since the federal government would have to continue spending an estimated $15 million to keep the Mariel excludables behind bars, and many millions more in legal fees. There was no guarantee against another massive and uncontrolled exodus.

The aftermath of the Mariel boatlift clearly showed that Castro's machinations to stimulate the exodus and to send "criminals" and "antisocials" to the United States were at least unethical, if not downright immoral. On those grounds alone, his actions were rightly condemned and repudiated by the international community. In light of the U.S. open-door policy for immigration from Cuba since 1959, however, Castro's action should be viewed as nothing more than politics as usual. Since that time, the United States had done everything possible to encourage immigration from Cuba in order to deprive the revolution of trained technicians and professionals, to hurt its image as a popular revolution, and to play a dubious human chip in the ongoing cold war.

The Mariel exodus proved that both sides could play refugee politics. By including several thousand "criminals" and "antisocials" in the "freedom flotilla," Castro sought to turn an embarrassing situation to his advantage. He reasoned that since those who committed crimes against Cuba's revolutionary government were hailed as heroes in the United States, the U.S. government should welcome the rest of Cuba's "heroes." In a sense, Castro was paying back an old debt for the revolution's loss in trained personnel and vessels through its defectors.

It is too early to reach definite conclusions on the Mariel experience. Nonetheless, fifteen years after the exodus and thirty-six years since Cuban refugees began arriving in the United States, several observations may be made. First, although the Mariel exodus created some problems for the Carter administration, the crisis was gradually deescalated, and eventually more than 80 percent of the Mariel entrants were resettled in the United States. Second, the Cuban migration to the United States from 1959 to 1980, especially trained personnel, hurt but did not destroy the Cuban revolution. Third, no objective and knowledgeable observers believe that Radio Martí will have a significant effect on Castro's power. Finally, Mariel, like Camarioca, should not be viewed as an isolated event. In the absence of a clear and mutually agreed upon migration policy, it could happen again.

If nothing else, the past thirty-five years should show the United States and Cuba that a war of refugees is neither profitable nor winnable by either side. Perhaps both countries will stop playing politics with the refugees and realize that a clear, rational, and just migration policy would benefit all involved.

Notes

1. Because the boatlift is so recent, press accounts are still the best source of information for the period. From April to August 1980, major newspapers like the *New York Times*, the *Washington Post*, and the *Miami Herald* carried at least one story a day on the boatlift. Cuban publications like *Granma*, *Bohemia*, and *Juventud Rebelde* are excellent sources for the boatlift's day-to-day operation and statistics on the number of incoming and outgoing vessels and people.

2. Peter Winn, "Is the Cuban Revolution in Trouble?" *Nation*, June 7, 1980, 682.

3. Ibid.

4. *Miami Herald*, August 28, 1980, 6a. See also June 3, 1980, 6a; and July 26, 1980, 6a.

5. Nick Nichols, "Castro's Revenge," *Washington Monthly*, March 1982, 40.

6. *U.S. News and World Report*, January 16, 1984, 27. For related stories on the Marielitos' criminality, see Paul Heath Hoeffel, "Fort Chaffee's Unwanted Cubans," *New York Times Magazine*, December 21, 1980, 31; "The Cuban Conundrum," *Newsweek*, September 29, 1980, 30; Linda R. Prout, "Racism, Cuban Style," *Village Voice*, September 2–8, 1981, 14.

7. *Miami Herald*, December 29, 1980, 6a.

8. For a good sampling of the pain and rejection felt by the stigmatized refugees, see *El Miami Herald*, June 5, 1980, 6; January 9, 1984, 14; January 14, 1981, 6; March 31, 1981, 8; June 12, 1981, 6.

9. Interview with Roberto Ramírez, Miami, Florida, May 30, 1985. This interview was conducted in strict confidentiality, and I was allowed to use it in this work only after gaining the subject's trust through a mutual friend. Roberto Ramírez's father visited his son in Miami on a two-month visa in 1983. To Ramírez's shock, his father returned to Cuba after only one week because "he could not stand life in this country." The subject's name has been changed to protect his privacy.

10. See *El Miami Herald*, June 25, 1980, 2; July 30, 1980, 2; August 23, 1980, 2; and *Miami Herald*, August 31, 1980, 1a.

11. *Newsweek*, September 1, 1980, 26.

12. *Miami Herald*, August 19, 1980, 6a. For details on the terrorist act that claimed the lives of seventy-three people, see Alicia Herrera, *Pusimos la bomba . . . y qué?* (Havana, 1981).

13. *Miami Herald*, August 19, 1980, 6a.

14. *New York Times*, May 28, 1983, 1. For more related stories on the second wave of hijackings, see *Miami Herald*, May 28, 1983, 1a; July 7, 1983, 1a; July 8, 1983, 16a; July 21, 1983, 30a.

15. Karen Shaw Kerpen, "Those Who Left: Two Years Later," *Cuba Times* 3 (Spring 1982): 1. See also Robert Bach, "The New Cuban Exodus," 22–25, 58–60; and Robert L. Bach and Timothy Triplett, "The Flotilla Entrants: Latest and Most Controversial," *Cuban Studies* 11–12 (July 1981–January 1982): 29–48.

16. Siro del Castillo, "Los Cubanos de antes y de ahora," *El Miami Herald*, March 12, 1981, 6. See also Siro del Castillo, "A Plea to Destigmatize Mariel," *Caribbean Review* 10: 7; Penny Lernoux, "The Miami Connection," *Nation*, February 18, 1984; idem., *In Banks We Trust* (New York, 1984).

17. *Miami Herald*, August 31, 1980, 2a.

18. Marta Harneker, "A Cuban Leader Answers Tough Questions," *Cuba Times* 2 (Spring 1981): 19, 21.

19. Ana María Radaelli, "Cubanos en el Peru. Dos años despues," *Cuba Internacional*, September 1982, pp. 30–33.

20. *Miami Herald*, November 24, 1983, 6g; *El Miami Herald*, November 6, 1983, 1.

21. *Miami Herald*, July 22, 1983, 15a.

22. *Miami Herald*, September 15, 1984, 4a.

23. *Miami Herald*, September 14, 1984, 4a.

24. *New York Times*, December 16, 1984, 1.

25. For summarized versions of Castro's "boat-packing," see Nick Nichols, "Castro's Revenge," *The Washington Monthly*, March 1982; "Castro's 'Crime Bomb' in the U.S.," *U.S. News and World Report*, January 16, 1984, 27–30.

26. Castro stated clearly in his May Day speech that "criminals" were being kept in safe custody in Cuba, but that "delinquents and ex-convicts" were being "encouraged" to leave the country. For full text of the speech, see Taber, ed., *Cuba's International Foreign Policy*, 271–90.

27. Interview with Raúl Quevedo, Miami, Florida, December 12, 1983.

28. Ibid. Quevedo was finally released from Fort Chaffee after an uncle sponsored him and brought him to Miami. Had he failed to communicate with that uncle, as he did for ten months, he would have been transferred to the Atlanta penitentiary to await deportation.

29. *El Miami Herald*, May 2, 1981, 6.

30. *Miami Herald*, July 8, 1983, 1a.

31. *Miami Herald*, August 31, 1983, 2a.

32. Ibid., September 15, 1983, 17a.

33. Ibid., November 13, 1983, 3d.

34. *New York Times*, December 11, 1983, 1. Alarcón Quesada and Kozak held three negotiation sessions before reaching the agreement. All sessions were held in New York City on July 12 and 13, July 31 to August 2, and November 28 to December 5, 1984.

35. *Department of State Bulletin*, February 1985, 44–45.

36. *Miami Herald*, December 16, 1984, 24a.

37. *Miami Herald*, December 20, 1984, 30a.

38. *New York Times*, February 22, 1985, 6.

39. *Miami Herald*, February 22, 1985, 1a.

40. *Granma*, February 22, 1985, 1.

41. *Miami Herald*, May 24, 1985, 27a.

42. Michael Taber, ed., *Fidel Castro: Speeches, 1984–85*, 237.

43. Ibid., 238.

44. *New York Times*, May 21, 1985, 6.

45. Howard Frederick, "La guerra radial: U.S./Cuba Radio Wars," *W.I.N.*, September 1983, 9.

46. Programs from Florida radio stations can be heard throughout Cuba. Upon my arrival in Cuba in 1979, I expected to be treated to a feast of Cuba's New Song movement, but was bombarded instead by top forty tunes from John Travolta to Chuck Mangione.

47. *Department of State Bulletin*, June 1983, 85.

48. Ibid., 85–86.

49. Franklin Siegel, "Treasury Impounds Cuban Periodicals," *Cuba Times* 2 (Fall 1981): 7–8; Kitty Stewart, "Welcome Back to the Free World," *Cuba Times* 5 (Fall 1984): 9–11. I had been receiving Cuban periodicals since August 1979—the source for much of this work—but my subscriptions were canceled by the Reagan administration's ban on Cuban periodicals.

50. *Miami Herald*, May 26, 1985, 24a.

51. *Miami Herald*, May 20, 1983, 1. See also Reagan's radio message to the Cuban people, *Department of State Bulletin*, March 1984, 3.

8

The Haitian and Central American Refugee Dilemma

We endorse public sanctuary as an ethical and legitimate response to the persecution of refugees and as a means of alerting the American people to the human cost of U.S. military policies in Central America. We believe dramatic witness is called for in the face of our government's disregard for the basic human rights of refugees.

American Friends Service Committee, January 1983

Contradictions and Double-Standards

DESPITE THE FLAWS AND CONTRADICTIONS in U.S. immigration procedures for Cubans, the state of Florida has coped admirably with the influx of nearly 1 million Cuban refugees since 1959. A multibillion-dollar federal aid program and the establishment of a strong social, economic, and political enclave in Miami effectively facilitated the group's adaptation. By 1980, however, Cubans were not the only refugees coming to Florida in large numbers. In addition to the 125,000 Mariel refugees, more than 3,000 Haitian "boat people" arrived illegally in south Florida during the first four months of the year, and an estimated 60,000 had entered the area illegally since 1972. The year 1980 also brought an increase in Central American asylum-seekers, namely Salvadorans, Guatemalans, and Nicaraguans escaping the political turmoil in their native countries.

The Immigration and Naturalization Service's initial response to the multiple refugee influx was strictly legalistic. Since the federal government did not have a status for persons seeking asylum from non-Communist nations, Haitians, Salvadorans, and Guatemalans were officially classified as "no status," denied asylum, and detained until deportation proceedings could be arranged.[1]

In stark contrast to the open-door, no-questions-asked immigration procedure applied to Cubans fleeing "Communist oppression," people seeking sanctuary from right-wing dictatorships friendly to the United States had to provide well-founded proof of their fear of persecution:

> Under a set of regulations left over from the Cold War, nearly anyone who comes from a Communist country or from the Middle East is a political refugee and receives favorable consideration for admission to the country . . . but those claiming asylum from right-wing governments, no matter how blatantly oppressive, have had a far more difficult time getting entry, since they must prove with documents and witnesses that they personally will be subject to persecution if they return.[2]

Under immigration law current in 1985, those who failed to prove a well-founded fear of persecution were classified as economic refugees and returned home. Such arbitrary classification hurt the Haitians more than any other group, since they emigrated from the poorest country in the Western Hemisphere. In Haiti two-thirds of the population barely survived on incomes of $140 a year, more than 80 percent of the people were illiterate, and the infant mortality rate was estimated at 130 to 150 per thousand, one of the highest in the world.[3] Viewed within the context of Haiti's extreme poverty, the economic refugee classification clearly applies to Haitians who would almost certainly improve their lot by emigrating to the United States. In Haiti under the dictatorship of Jean-Claude Duvalier, however, economics and politics were closely linked.

Haiti's government and economy have been dominated by one family since 1957, when François (Papa Doc) Duvalier was elected president of the republic. Duvalier, who proclaimed himself "president for life" in 1964, established a corrupt dictatorship that permeated every level of society. The dictator's security force, the Tontons Macoutes, systematically assassinated political opponents and forced bribes from even the poorest peasants.

François Duvalier's regime drove thousands of Haitians, especially the educated and professional elite, into exile. Although political exile was not new for upper-class Haitians, under Duvalier the exiles' numbers and class composition changed drastically. Alex Stepick observed in 1982:

> Political opponents of a new Haitian president have always seen the wisdom of leaving Haiti. However, the past 23 years [1959–82] have seen all levels of Haitian society successively feel the need to leave. The first to leave were the upper elite who stood as a direct threat to Papa Doc's regime. Then came the black middle class (around 1963) who found the brutality of the Duvalier regime and the lack of personal and economic security unacceptable. Next, many of the urban lower classes departed. The primary United States destination of these groups has been New York City where there are presently between 200 and 300 thousand Haitians.[4]

When Papa Doc died in 1971, his nineteen-year-old son Jean-Claude (Baby Doc) Duvalier inherited the lifelong presidency and continued ruling Haiti autocratically. Two years after the second Duvalier took over, Amnesty International, the Nobel Peace Prize–winning human rights organization, compared Haitian prisons to Nazi concentration camps: "The variety of torture to which the detainee is subjected is incredible: clubbing to death, maiming of the genitals, food deprivations to the point of starvation, and the insertion of red-hot pokers into the back passage. . . . In fact, these prisons are death traps."[5]

Governmental corruption under the second Duvalier persisted at such a high level that one observer characterized Haitian society as a "kleptocracy" ruled by a government of thieves. An often-cited example of corruption and the elite's disregard for public funds was the $100,000 salary that Michelle Bennet, Baby Doc's wife, drew every month for her duties as "Mrs. President."[6] In addition, there were innumerable stories about hundreds of millions of dollars that somehow "disappeared" or were "lost" from International Monetary Fund loans and other international lending institutions. Still, the U.S. government continued subsidizing the regime with generous loans and grants and, in 1982, the Reagan administration boosted U.S. aid to Haiti from $30 million to $50 million.[7]

Duvalier's stranglehold on the government and economy of Haiti and the regime's extreme brutality and corruption oppressed the Haitian people both politically and economically. According to Reverend Gerard Jean-Juste, director of the Haitian Refugee Center in Miami, the situation was further exacerbated by U.S. support for the dictatorship:

> In Haiti, life is a problem. We could solve the problem by improving the situation at home. Right now fifty percent of all children die before reaching four years of age. Ninety percent of all people do not receive a regular supply of piped water. The illiteracy rate is eighty-five percent. Forty percent of the people have no lodging at all. . . . There are thirty-five prisons for each high school in Haiti. For each teacher, there are 189 soldiers. We have a hellish situation in Haiti. How come Mr. Reagan wants to back up this government that has been there for twenty-four years and keeps getting worse?[8]

While the political situation has certainly improved since the ouster of the Duvalier regime in 1986, Haiti's economy remains extremely weak and grossly mismanaged. Twenty-nine years of repression and corruption cannot be wiped out overnight, and for Haiti this means an uncertain future at best. Thus, the following observation, made by an ex-political prisoner in 1982 remains valid today: "Politics and everyday life in Haiti cannot be separated. A man can casually say that he is hungry and that can be misconstrued to mean he is criticizing the government's mismanagement of funds, therefore, leading to his arrest."[9]

Unlike the Cubans who came to the United States after 1959 to flee a Communist government unfriendly to the United States, the Haitians came from a government friendly to this nation. Thus the dilemma: if the United States welcomed Haitian refugees on political grounds, it would have verified Duvalier's brutal repression of his people, a favorite U.S. charge against Castro. Admitting Haitians on economic grounds would set a precedent for millions worldwide who could claim the same right. Rejecting the Haitians on both grounds, as has been the case so far, would underline a double-standard on granting asylum vis-à-vis the Cubans and other refugees escaping leftist regimes.

The double-standard was most evident during the Mariel boatlift of 1980, when 125,000 Cubans were welcomed to the United States with "open hearts and open arms," while an estimated 25,000 Haitians, who came into south Florida during the same period and in similar fashion, were denied asylum and threatened with deportation. To avoid discrimination charges and to defuse a crisis, President Carter created a new classification, "Cuban/Haitian Entrant (status pending)," to allow both Cubans and Haitians who had entered the United States before January 1, 1981, to remain in the country on a two-year trial basis.

Carter's "entrant" solution benefited Haitians in the short run but affected only those who were in the United States before 1981. Nothing was said or done about subsequent Haitian entrants, who continued sailing into south Florida at the rate of 10,000 a year.

The Haitian "Boat People"

On December 12, 1972, the first boatload of sixty-five Haitians landed in Miami, and by 1979, between 5,000 and 10,000 risked their lives each year in desperate attempts to reach Florida. By 1980 more than 1,000 a month were braving the rough 800-mile voyage to south Florida in leaky wooden sailboats.[10] Leaving everything behind, they defied death at sea and on land (if caught by Haitian authorities) to reach the "promised land," as they fondly called the United States.

Those who survived the voyage, which sometimes took thirty or more days, were received with hostility in the United States. From 1972 to 1980 they were allowed to stay in the country. Unlike the Cubans, who received full governmental support until they settled, Haitians were left on their own and had to depend on charitable organizations, churches, and Miami's black community. The new Haitian refugees were very different from the professionals and skilled workers who had migrated to the United States and Canada during the 1960s: they were uneducated, unskilled, overwhelmingly black, and speakers of Creole, the unique language that blends French, Spanish, English and several African dialects and is spoken by 90 percent of Haitians. These were the poor of the poorest nation in the Western Hemisphere. It would not be easy for them to adjust to life in the United States, but they preferred anything to life under the Duvalier dictatorship. Moreover, once a Haitian left his country, a return meant probable death or a long prison sentence, since the government regarded emigration as a treasonous act and an insult to the Duvalier family.[11]

For most Haitians who managed to reach Florida after May 18, 1981, life in the "promised land" turned into a nightmare. On that day, the Immigration and Naturalization Service abandoned its policy of releasing Haitian refugees into the community and began detaining them at Camp Krome, a former missile base in North Dade County.[12] The new detention program underlined yet another contradiction in U.S. immigration policy toward Haitians. Unlike the 1,050 Cuban excludables held in federal prisons, Haitians were not criminals in the ordinary sense. Their only crime was to seek political asylum in a country long recognized as a sanctuary for oppressed peoples.

Detention was only part of the Reagan administration's plan to curb immigration from Haiti. On September 29, 1981, the president issued an executive order authorizing the Coast Guard to patrol the high seas and intercept foreign vessels carrying "migrants coming to the United States by sea, without necessary entry documents."[13] The interdiction program was a joint U.S.-Haiti effort for which the United States provided all the equipment necessary to patrol the fifty-mile wide Windward Passage between Cuba and Haiti: the 378-foot cutter *Hamilton*, two helicopters, a C-130 reconnaissance plane, and the $1 million monthly cost of the program. In return, Haiti provided Creole-English interpreters and immigration officers to supervise the refugees' return to Haiti.[14]

The program had three problems. First, it was unable to stop all emigration from Haiti. Second, it was not very cost-effective: the program claimed to have turned back only, 3,337 Haitians between October 1981 and December 1984. This meant that for each returned Haitian, the United States paid approximately $116,870.[15] Third, the program triggered a loud and anguished outcry against U.S. immigration policies and practices.

In an angry but well-reasoned column published in the *Miami Herald*, Marvin E. Frankel, chairman of the New York-based Lawyers Committee for International Human Rights, condemned the interdiction on moral and legal grounds:

> It is declared explicitly in this disgraceful pact that our Coast Guard people are required to search out and deal with violations of "appropiate" Haitian laws. So United States ships and Coast Guardsmen are officially in the law-enforcement business on behalf of what has been described by the International Commission of Jurists as the most ruthless and oppressive regime in the world. . . . Beyond the ignoring of the Refugee Act, the Haitian interdiction program violates the Constitutional gurantee of due process of law that governs all officials, high and low, in or out of uniform. In our

democracy, officials have to have legal authority before they can grab and deal forcefully with things, let alone with people. [16]

Similar indignation was expressed by Reverend Jean-Juste, who called interdiction "a clear violation of international law and the United Nations' treaty and protocol on refugees." Congressional Black Caucus leader Walter Fauntroy called the plan "racist" and "ideologically biased," since the administration's refugee allocations favored anti-Communists from Indochina and Eastern Europe and disregarded the human rights of black refugees. [17]

While the interdiction debate raged, the detainees at Camp Krome swelled to 1,200, making the camp extremely cramped and tense. Then the federal government decided to transfer Krome's entire population plus another 1,300 Haitians (detained at fourteen refugee detention centers around the country) to Fort Drum in upstate New York. The 107,265-acre army base—30 miles south of the Canadian border, with an average snowfall of twelve feet and winter temperatures that plunged to minus 30° F—was sure to confuse and traumatize Haitians accustomed to a tropical climate and year-long temperatures ranging from 70° to 90° F.

Like the interdiction program, the federal government's decision to relocate the detained Haitians elicited an equally angry reaction from human rights activists and civic leaders. Ira Kurzban, an attorney for the Haitian Refugee Center of Miami and the National Emergency Civil Liberties Committee, accused the government of putting the refugees "in a completely alien environment, separate from lawyers, with the idea of getting them voluntarily to return to Haiti, circumventing the legal process." Miami Mayor Maurice Ferré angrily denounced the Reagan administration's steps as racist: "What the federal government is doing, is sending a message to Haitians that, if they come here, it won't be easy, both with the interdiction program and by keeping them in places that aren't comfortable. . . . We have to start closing down our borders, but we can't be racists, saying we welcome whites and don't want blacks." [18]

Detained Haitians dramatized their plight by staging peaceful hunger strikes at Camp Krome in Miami, at the federal prison in Lexington, Kentucky, and at Fort Allen, Puerto Rico. Their actions were supported by solidarity demonstrations outside the facilities by the Haitian community and concerned citizens. [19] Among those who expressed solidarity with the Haitians was the Reverend Jesse

Jackson, founder of the Chicago-based Operation PUSH (People United to Save Humanity) and presidential candidate in 1984, who visited Camp Krome and appealed to the world's conscience on the Haitians' behalf. Jackson accused the Reagan administration of using a double-standard against Haitians because they were black: "Whites are greeted by the Statue of Liberty and blacks are deleted by the statute of limitations." He was also critical of Pope John Paul's seeming disregard for black human rights: "While the pope has offered to sacrifice himself to end the unrest in Poland, the Vatican has maintained a deafening silence regarding mistreatment of blacks in Haiti and South Africa."[20]

As the Haitians' plight gained publicity and support, their battle to stay in the United States moved into the nation's courtrooms. In December 1981, the Haitian Refugee Center of Miami filed a class-action suit against the federal government for the release of all detained Haitians in the United States and Puerto Rico. United States 11th District Circuit Court of Appeals Judge Eugene P. Spellman responded to the suit by appointing a committee of lawyers to investigate the case and to recruit free legal representation for the Haitians at their asylum hearings.[21] On June 18, 1982, Spellman ruled that the immigration policy was administratively flawed and illegal. The Immigration and Naturalization Service, he ruled, had devised and implemented a policy of detention in violation of federal administrative rules, and all Haitians detained under President Reagan's May 18, 1981, executive order were to be released as soon as possible. As a result, 1,771 Haitians were released from Krome and other detention centers.[22]

Spellman's decision was hailed as a triumph for fairness by human rights activists and, of course, the detainees. Some citizens questioned the ruling's soundness, however, since detention had been declared illegal not on moral or philosophical grounds, but on a legal technicality. In an editorial praising Spellman's decision, titled "Thank You, Judge," the *Miami Herald* expressed concerns over the Justice Department's ability to continue detaining Haitians under new, legal regulations:

> It is ironic that a technicality should be the instrument that severs the chains of shame by which the United States Government has kept these Haitians in their inhuman bondage, some for almost a year. It will not be ironic if the Justice Department attempts to reforge those chains by following Federal rules and reinstituting

this discredited and dishonorable policy. It will be unconstitutional.[23]

Those who questioned the Spellman decision were proven right just a few weeks after the ruling. Although the Immigration and Naturalization Service released most Haitians in its custody, it stepped up its interdiction policy, stopping 425 Haitian boats on the high seas and taking 1,733 would-be refugees back to Haiti from 1982 to 1984. In the meantime, the Justice Department continued its intense appeals to reverse the Spellman decision, which it finally accomplished on February 28, 1984. The full 11th District Court of Appeals ruled that detention of excludable aliens fell within the government's authority to control its borders. The court further ruled that illegal aliens captured at the border had no constitutional rights and could be detained indefinitely.[24]

Haitian refugees suffered an equally damaging defeat in November 1984, when the Immigration and Naturalization Service announced that the 125,000 Cubans who had entered the United States during the Mariel boatlift were eligible for legal status and U.S. citizenship under the Cuban Adjustment Act of 1966. The law, which had been specially designed for Cubans who came to the United States during the Camarioca boatlift of 1965, did not apply to the 30,000 Haitians granted entrant status in 1980.[25]

Many people, including Reverend Gerard Jean-Juste, believed the Immigration and Naturalization Service's decision was based on racism. He contended that "the Immigration and Naturalization Service has a tradition of being a racist institution and would be more interested in granting residency for other ethnic groups."[26] The *Miami Herald* expressed similar feelings:

> INS has the legal authority to grant the Cubans legal residency under the Cuban Adjustment Act of 1966. No such law exists for Haitians. Thus INS acted correctly, even though 2½ years late, when it decided to grant the Cubans that which the law provides.
> . . . Once the decision is put into effect regarding the Cubans, the issue becomes a matter of conscience regarding the Haitians. That is what the Carter Administration invited when it created the status of Cuban-Haitian entrant in 1980. The entrant status is on shaky legal ground, but the argument for treating the Cubans and Haitians equally is morally unassailable. This country cannot accept a racist immigration policy.[27]

The status question raised by President Carter in 1980 had come full circle and, as in the past, Cubans received preferential treatment, leaving Haitians in a state of legal limbo, humiliation, and fear.

The Central American Refugee Influx

Haitians were not the only refugees having trouble proving their fears of persecution to the Immigration and Naturalization Service. From 1979 to 1985, more than 500,000 Salvadorans, Guatemalans, and Nicaraguans entered the United States in search of political asylum.

Central American refugees are similar to Haitians in several ways. First, like the Haitians they claimed to be fleeing political repression and government violence in their country, but they are also emigrating from extremely poor countries. Thus the Immigration and Naturalization Service has classified them as economic refugees and refused them asylum on political grounds. Second, Central American refugees from El Salvador and Guatemala (but not Nicaragua) are also escaping countries whose governments the United States fully supports; for the United States to admit large numbers of Salvadoran and Guatemalan political refugees would be at least an embarrassment to U.S. foreign policy. Third, in Central America, as in Haiti, politics and economics cannot be separated, since the former strongly influence the latter.

A major difference between Haitian and Central American refugees concerned the state of belligerency in Central America: civil war in El Salvador, widespread insurgency in Guatemala, and a U.S.–backed counterrevolutionary war in Nicaragua. Another major difference between the two groups was race. While Haitians are overwhelmingly black, Central Americans are overwhelmingly Mestizo and Amerindian. Finally, but perhaps most important, Central Americans were not coming to the United States only to escape the political situation in their respective countries, they were going anywhere that would be safer. According to the Salvadoran Humanitarian Aid, Research and Education Foundation, by the end of 1982, more than 10 percent of its population had fled El Salvador. Seventy thousand migrated to Guatemala, 120,000 to Mexico, 30,000 went to Honduras, 22,000 to Nicaragua, and thousands more to Costa Rica, Panama, and Belize. In addition, more than 200,000 had been displaced by the war inside El Salvador.[28]

The causes for the Central American refugee exodus were many, but most observers agree that political violence perpetrated by repressive governments stands out as the most significant factor. Patricia Weiss Fagen points to the relationship between the Reagan administration's continued support of those governments and the flow of refugees:

> With respect to politically motivated exiles, U.S. foreign policy has contributed to the very flows that are now so difficult to stem. The Reagan Administration continues to support governments that violate human rights, fail to provide for the basic needs of their citizens, and repeatedly unleash security-force violence against their civilian populations. Such governments, in effect, drive people who otherwise would remain in their countries into exile.[29]

The United States plays an important role in the Central American conflicts and since 1979 has provided more than $2 billion in military aid to the governments of El Salvador and Honduras. In addition, the Reagan administration has gradually resumed military aid to the Guatemalan government, which was cut off in 1977 when Amnesty International declared it one of the most repressive regimes in the world. Finally, the administration, with congressional approval, supports the efforts of the rebel army (contras) trying to overthrow the Sandinista government of Nicaragua.[30]

Nicaragua presents a particularly difficult problem for the federal government's immigration policy. Although the administration openly finances and supports the Sandinistas' enemies, Nicaragua is not a Communist nation and still has diplomatic relations with the United States. Thus when Nicaraguans claiming to be fleeing Sandinista repression apply for political asylum in the United States, the Immigration and Naturalization Service is presented with a difficult dilemma.

The situation took a bizarre turn in 1984 when it was discovered that more than 7,000 Nicaraguan draft-dodgers had entered Miami illegally and kept coming at the rate of 100 a month, because their parents feared "they would be killed in combat with CIA-backed rebels."[31] Under the Refugee Act of 1980, conscription is not considered political persecution, so each draft-dodger's case would have to be considered individually; if the law was applied in accord with the apparent intent of its conscription provision, their requests would be denied. As the *Miami Herald* pointed out in an editorial, the Nicaraguan draft-dodgers' case could establish dangerous precedents for other Nicaraguan and Central American refugees:

> More than 50 percent of Nicaragua's population is under age 16, and both males and females face conscription. Granting political asylum for those fleeing conscription would be a dangerous precedent. It might entice thousands of Nicaraguans to flee to South Florida too. . . . Furthermore, a magnanimous gesture giving all the young Nicaraguans permission to stay here might prompt charges of favoritism by the lawyers for 500,000 Salvadorans—many of them fleeing civil war at home.[32]

The editorial also blamed the administration for the new influx of illegal refugees, and called on it and Congress to stop playing politics with immigration policy:

> It's ironic that this streamlet of Nicaraguans might never have existed had not the Reagan Administration let the CIA hire an army of 15,000 contras to try to overthrow Nicaragua's Sandinista regime. Absent that threat, the Sandinistas might not have had to draft young men and women into their army. . . . As the administration and Congress consider renewed financing for the contras, they must weigh the effects that U.S. policy in Central America can have on illegal migration to this country. The inexorable ties between foreign policy and immigration issues must be recognized before any progress can be made in U.S. efforts to control illegal migration.[33]

In June 1985, the U.S. Congress approved $27 million to continue the Reagan administration's efforts to overthrow the Sandinista government, but failed to pass immigration reform. Once again, the legal status of more than 500,000 Central American refugees was left in limbo.[34]

The Sanctuary Movement

On March 24, 1982, John Fife, pastor of the Southside United Presbyterian Church in Tucson, Arizona, declared that church a sanctuary for Central American refugees escaping government-sponsored violence in their countries. The First Unitarian Church in Los Angeles, the University Lutheran Chapel in San Francisco, Luther Place Memorial Church in Washington, D.C., and an independent bible church in Long Island, New York, followed suit on the same day.[35] This coordinated action launched what has come to be known as the Sanctuary Movement, which has developed into a loose network of more than 75,000 religious people and approximately 250 churches, synagogues, and Quaker meetinghouses that have declared their places of worship to be sanctuary sites.[36]

Outraged by the rapidly rising death toll of civilians in El Salvador and Guatemala, and by more than 50,000 Salvadoran deportations in 1981, sanctuary activists, guided by conscience and religious belief, decided to shelter undocumented Central Americans in their homes and churches regardless of the consequences. Their faith and resolve is reflected in the words of a defense offered in court by indicted church workers:

> The earth itself is to become a sanctuary. This convenant forms us into a people of many nations, cultures, and creeds—a people that the Christians among us sometimes call the church! Protective community with the persecuted is an inalienable requirement of the convenant to hallow the earth. And the intercongregational provisions of sanctuary for Central American refugees is simply the practice of our faith as a covenant people. This means that we cannot agree to ignore any person who asks for our help to escape torture and murder. Many of us, if ordered by the State to do so, might sacrifice a pinch of incense to Caesar, but we cannot sacrifice the lives of Central American refugees. . . . We pray for the strength to love and the courage to remain true to our faith—that the Kingdom may come on earth, in our lives and during our days, and in the lives of all the covenant peoples.[37]

In addition to practicing their religious beliefs, sanctuary workers were also concerned about the U.S. role in the Central American conflicts and strongly criticized the Reagan administration's intervention in the area. When the Riverside Church became New York City's first sanctuary in September 1984, Reverend William Sloan Coffin, Jr., a veteran anti-Vietnam war activist, told his parishioners:

> It is a bleak but realistic assessment to say that our government intends to escalate further its intervention in Central American countries. Therefore it behooves us North American Christians to realize now what the German churches learned too late some forty years ago: that it is not enough to resist with confession. We must confess with resistance.[38]

Sanctuary workers maintain that their actions are legal, and that the United States government acts illegally by refusing to grant asylum to those fleeing the warfare and death squads of Central America. They argue that the Salvadoran and Guatemalan undocumented aliens are eligible for political asylum under the Refugee Act of 1980, since indiscriminate political violence in their country of origin justifies a "well-founded fear of persecution." Furthermore, the Geneva Convention states that governments must allow private humanitarian agencies or individuals to protect refugees from untimely repatriation.[39] For those reasons, many sanctuary workers interpret the U.S. refusal to provide protection for Central American refugees as a violation of domestic and international law.

The U.S. government responded to the Sanctuary Movement with a crackdown against its most active members. On January 23, 1985, John Fife and fifteen others were arraigned in Tucson, Arizona, and charged with seventy-one counts, including conspiracy and harboring and transporting illegal aliens.[40] The government's case is based almost entirely on about one hundred tape recordings, many of them made by paid Immigration and Naturalization Service informants who took concealed recording equipment into Bible-study classes and prayer services in churches involved in the Sanctuary Movement.[41]

Despite the Sanctuary Movement's political awareness of the Central American situation and its attacks on the Reagan administration's foreign policy, the movement is primarily religious and humanitarian in nature. As Reverend Philip Wheaton, an Episcopal priest and coordinator of the Metropolitan D.C. Sanctuary Committee, said: "This is a middle class, white, Catholic-Protestant movement. [Sanctuary workers] are people responding to a humanitarian concern."[42] Sanctuary activists are committed to a cause they consider just, humane, and in perfect accordance with their religious beliefs.

The Sanctuary Movement provided a short-term solution to stop the arbitrary and unjust deportation of hundreds of Central American refugees. Just the fact that the movement existed and gained widespread support was a clear indication that something was profoundly wrong with the U.S. government's handling of refugees. Challenged by a determined religious community, the Immigration and Naturalization Service and the Justice Department faced the unpleasant and unpopular task of prosecuting U.S. citizens for the "crime" of helping a neighbor in need.

Notes

1. Haitian Task Force, "Haitian Refugees in Florida: Background Information," Office of the Governor of Florida, October 25, 1984.
2. Kevin Krajick, "Refugees Adrift: Barred from America's Shores," *Saturday Review*, October 27, 1979, 17.
3. U.S. Department of State, "Background Notes: Haiti," April 1977. For more on social conditions in Haiti, see Robert J. Tata, *Haiti: Land of Poverty* (Washington, D. C., 1982); Robert I. Rolberg, *Haiti: The Politics of Squalor* (Boston, 1971); Charles Gerard Pierre, *Problemas dominico-haitianos y el Caribe* (Mexico, 1978); James G. Leyburn, *The Haitian People* (New Haven, 1966); Robert D. Heinl, *Written in Blood: The Story of the Haitian People, 1492–1971* (Boston, 1978); Thomas O. Ott, *The Haitian Revolution, 1789–1904* (Knoxville, 1973); Hans Schmidt, *The United States Occupation of Haiti, 1915–1934* (New Brunswick, 1971); Arthur C. Millspaugh, *Haiti Under American Control, 1915–1934* (Boston, 1931); and Bernard Diederich, *Papa Doc: The Truth About Haiti Today* (New York, 1969).
4. Alex Stepick, "The New Haitian Exodus: The Flight From Terror and Poverty," *Caribbean Review* 11 (Winter 1982): 16. For more on the migration of Haitian professionals in the 1960s and early 1970s, see Michel S. La Guerre, *American Odyssey: Haitians in New York City* (Ithaca, 1984); and Jervis Anderson, "Haitians of New York," *New Yorker*, March 31, 1975, 50–55.
5. Quoted in Stepick, "The New Haitian Exodus," 56.
6. Ibid., 17.
7. *Newsweek*, February 1, 1982, 27.
8. *New York Times*, November 12, 1983, 13.
9. Stepick, "The New Haitian Exodus," 56.
10. Florida Impact, "Haitian Refugees," *Prepare*, March 1981, 5. See also U.S. Congress, House of Representatives, Committee on the Judiciary, Subcommittee on Immigration, Citizenship, and International Law, *Hearings on Haitian Emigration*, 94th Cong., 2d sess., 1976; U.S. Congress, House of Representatives, Committee on the Judiciary, *Hearings on the Caribbean Refugee Crisis: Cubans and Haitians*, 96th Cong., 2d sess., 1980.
11. *Newsweek*, June 2, 1980, 53.
12. *Miami Herald*, May 19, 1981, 1a. See also Michelle Bogre, "Haitian Refugees," *Migration Today* 7 (4): 9–11; Ira Gollobin, "Haitian Boat People and Equal Justice Under Law: Background and Perspective," *Migration Today* 7 (4): 40–41; and Bryan O. Walsh, "Haitian in Miami," *Migration Today* 7 (4): 42–44.
13. *Miami Herald*, October 2, 1981, 6a.
14. *Guardian*, October 21, 1981, 16.
15. *Miami Herald*, December 5, 1984, 1a. The $116,870 estimate is my own, arrived at by dividing the $39 million budget by 3,337, the number of returned Haitians. The dollar amount could be much higher if there were budget increases or overruns in the thirty-nine months.
16. *Miami Herald*, May 28, 1983, 25a.

17. *Guardian* (London), October 21, 1981, 16.

18. *New York Times*, November 12, 1981, 13.

19. *New York Times*, December 25, 1981, 10.

20. *Miami Herald*, January 3, l982, 16a. For more on the Jackson visit and the community support for his efforts, see *Miami Herald*, January 2, 1982, 1a.

21. *Miami Herald*, June 19, 1982, 1a.

22. Stepick, "The New Haitian Exodus," 56.

23. *Miami Herald*, July 1, 1982, 24a.

24. Ibid., July 1, 1984, 16a.

25. *New York Times*, February 12, 1984, 1; *Miami Herald*, November 20, 1984, 1a; and February 16, 1984, 30a.

26. *Guardian* (London), October 31, 1984, 6.

27. *Miami Herald*, February 16, 1984, 30a.

28. Salvadoran Humanitarian Aid, Research and Education Foundation, "El Salvador: Refugees in Crisis" 1 (November–December 1982): 4. For testimonies by the refugees themselves, see Susanne Jonas, Ed McCaughon, and Elizabeth Sutherland Martines, eds., *Guatemala: Tyranny on Trial: Testimony of the Permanent People's Tribunal* (San Francisco, 1984); Marlene Dixon, ed., *On Trial: Reagan's War Against Nicaragua: Testimony of the Permanent People's Tribunal* (San Francisco, 1985).

29. Patricia Weiss Fagen, "Latin American Refugees: Problems of Mass Migration and Mass Asylum," in Richard Newfarmer, ed., *From Gunboat to Diplomacy* (Baltimore 1984), 229.

30. The current conflicts in Central America and the U.S. role in them have generated a rich literature. The following titles provide a wide range of perspectives: Edelberto Torres Rivas, ed., *Centro América: Hoy* (Mexico City, 1975); Lester D. Langley, *Central America, The Real Stakes: Understanding Central America Before It's Too Late* (New York, 1985); Mario Menendez Rodríguez, *El Salvador: Una auténtica guerra civil* (San José, Costa Rica, 1981); Robert Armstrong and Janet Shenk, *El Salvador: The Face of Revolution* (Boston, 1982); Rafael Menjívar, *El Salvador: El eslabón más pequeño* (San José, Costa Rica, 1980); Rafael Menjívar, ed., *La inversión extranjera en Centroamérica* (San José, Costa Rica, 1981); Alan Richard White, *The Morass: United States Intervention in Central America* (New York, 1984); Walter LaFeber, *Inevitable Revolutions: The United States in Central America* (New York, 1983); Richard Bonner, *Weakness and Deceit: U.S. Policy in El Salvador* (New York, 1984); Adolfo Gilly, *La nueva Nicaragua: anti-imperialismo y lucha de clases* (Mexico City, 1980); John A. Booth, *The End and the Beginning: The Nicaraguan Revolution* (Boulder, 1982).

31. *Miami Herald*, August 2, 1984, 1b.

32. *Miami Herald*, September 15, 1984, 26a.

33. Ibid.

34. On June 12, 1985, the U.S. Congress approved $27 million in "humanitarian aid" to the rebels trying to overthrow the Nicaraguan government (*New York Times* June 13, 1985, 1). The Simpson-Mazolli immigration reform bill was defeated during the same congressional session.

35. "Conspiracy of Compassion," *Sojourners*, March 1985, 17.

36. *In These Times*, September 4–10, 1985, 17.

37. Joyce Hollyday, "A Spirit of Resolve," *Sojourners*, March 1985, 10.

38. *Guardian* (London), October 31, 1984, 6.

39. Ibid.

40. *Sojourners*, March 1985, 14.

41. Nat Hentoff, "Snoops in the Pews," *Progressive*, August 1985, 25. For

more details on the government's spying against the Sanctuary Movement, see Sandy Tolan and Carol Ann Bassett, "Informers in the Sanctuary Movement," *Nation*, July 20–27, 1985, 40–44; Allan Nairn, "Assault on Sanctuary: A Church Rallies to Protect a Salvadoran Whistleblower," *Progressive*, August 1985, 20–23; Moe Snell, "Attack on Sanctuary," *In These Times*, October 2–8, 1985, 12–13; *Basta* (National Newsletter of the Chicago Religious Task Force on Central America), April 1985.

42. *Miami Herald*, October 22, 1985, 8a.

9

From Mariel to Guantánamo

Cubans must know that the only way to come to the United States is
by applying in Cuba. . . . They [those who arrive in the U.S. illegally]
will be placed in exclusion proceedings, and treated as are all illegal
migrants from other countries.

U.S. Attorney General Janet Reno, May 2, 1995

U.S. Immigration in the Post-Cold War Era

THE CLINTON ADMINISTRATION'S DECISION to stop granting Cuban migrants automatic political asylum in the United States
marked the end of an era of unrestricted admission and preferential
treatment of Cubans based strictly on political considerations. The
May 2, 1995, decision radically changed a thirty-six-year-old policy
designed to welcome Cubans to the United States as political refugees in order to discredit and undermine Fidel Castro's revolution.
Overnight and without warning, Cubans arriving illegally in the
U.S. were no longer welcomed, nor even considered special.

The Cuban community in the United States reacted vociferously
and with great indignation to the policy and status change, accusing
the Clinton administration of treason and staging demonstrations
and acts of civil disobedience in Miami, Union City, and Washington, D.C. The Cuban government, on the other hand, praised Clinton for seriously trying to normalize the migration flow between
the two countries. In reality, the administration's policy shift had
more to do with international political changes of recent years and
U.S. domestic policies than with the thirty-six-year-old political
war between the U.S. and Cuba.[1]

With the end of the Cold War in 1989 and the disintegration of the Soviet Union in 1991, Cuba's importance in the U.S. foreign policy agenda declined considerably. The U.S.S.R.'s demise brought severe economic dislocation and hardship to Cuba, thus limiting the Cuban government's capacity to challenge U.S. hegemony in Latin America. In that context, the Clinton administration was willing to keep up the Cold War, anti-Castro rhetoric, while exploring diplomatic channels that would lead to a normal and controlled migratory process from Cuba.

Like Cuba, Central America—the region of the world that was considered most vital to U.S. national security during the Reagan and Bush administrations—also lost its priority position in the post–Cold War U.S. foreign policy agenda. In Nicaragua, where the U.S. spent several billion dollars trying to overthrow the Sandinistas, the F.S.L.N. lost the presidential elections of 1990 and has been out of power since. In El Salvador, where the U.S. supported the right-wing military dictatorship responsible for a twelve-year civil war that resulted in 75,000 deaths, the F.M.L.N. signed a peace treaty with the government in 1992 and formed a political party that has so far failed to gain power through the electoral process. In Guatemala, Latin America's oldest war continues with the U.S supporting the government. The rebel movement has failed to overthrow the military-dominated civilian government, but peace talks have been going on since 1990.[2]

The political changes in Nicaragua and El Salvador had an immediate effect on the lives of more than one million Nicaraguans and Salvadorans who came to the United States during the 1980s to escape U.S.-sponsored wars in their native countries. Unlike Cubans, who under the Cuban Adjustment Act of 1966 became eligible for permanent legal residence after one year in the U.S., most Nicaraguans and Salvadorans only had temporary work permits, renewable every twelve months. As soon as the wars were over, the I.N.S. stopped issuing new work permits, and ordered most Nicaraguans and Salvadorans to return to their respective countries voluntarily or face deportation.[3]

Another group that was also ordered to return to its country of origin was the nearly 15,000 Haitians detained in the U.S. naval base at Guantánamo Bay, Cuba, and an estimated 150,000 living in the U.S. with only temporary work permits. Haiti was politically "stabilized" in September 1994, after the U.S. negotiated the departure of General Raoul Cédras's military government and guaranteed the return of exiled President Jean-Bertrand Aristide.

Haitians had always been negatively affected by the double standards of U.S. immigration policy (see chapter 8). Arbitrarily and falsely labeled as economic refugees, denied the opportunity to claim political asylum, the Haitian migration to the United States virtually disappeared during Aristide's eight months of democratic government. Yet, at the height of political violence and military repression following Aristide's overthrow in 1991, the Bush administration interdicted and deported more than 34,000 Haitians back to their military persecutors.[4]

The move to deport Nicaraguans, Salvadorans, and Haitians received strong public support from growing anti-immigrant groups in the United States and the rising sentiment that immigration from Latin America must be controlled, even if it meant sealing off the U.S. border with Mexico. Spearheaded by the English Only movement of the 1980s, which advocated a constitutional amendment to make English the official language of the United States, the anti-immigrant forces gained strength and momentum with the Republicans' victory in the 1994 congressional elections and the approval of Proposition 187 in California. This new law calls for the elimination of all public social services to undocumented immigrants, including health care, elementary and secondary education, and post-secondary education.

Under the slogan of "Save Our State" (S.O.S), California Governor Pete Wilson falsely but successfully blamed a wide range of economic, social, and political problems on the state's large Mexican immigrant population. The governor hoped to use his unscrupulous anti-immigrant campaign on the national level to help him win the presidency in 1996.

The rapid spread of anti-immigrant sentiment in the United States, along with the end of the Cold War, transformed the issue of Cuban immigration to the U.S. from one of vital importance for U.S. foreign policy to simply one of many ordinary and rather insignificant domestic political issues. These factors must be taken into consideration in order to understand President Clinton's policy decisions of August 1994 and May 1995.

The Cuba Issue in U.S. Politics

After several years of low visibility, the Cuba issue returned to the center stage of U.S. political debate in 1992. The return was propelled mainly by the disintegration of the Soviet Union, the fall of Communism in Eastern Europe, and the "official" end of the Cold War. The U.S. no longer had to worry about the "Soviet threat," so it again turned its attention to the "Cuban threat." The United States accused Cuba and Castro of going against the tide of democracy engulfing Latin America, instigating and supporting political subversion in the region, drug trafficking, and violating the human rights of Cubans. Ironically, the U.S., which for more than thirty years had justified its attacks against Cuba for the latter's close alliance with the Soviet Union, now urged the Cuban government to emulate the Soviet model for change.

1992 was also a presidential election year in the United States, and as in past presidential elections, the Cuba issue figured prominently in the campaign. Just a few months before the elections, U.S. Representative Robert Torricelli (D-NJ), Chairman of the House Western Hemisphere Subcommittee, proposed a bill designed to tighten the U.S. economic embargo against Cuba and to strengthen the prospects for democracy in the island. The "Cuban Democracy Act" (CDA, also known as the Torricelli bill) was intended to hasten Castro's fall from power, and like other strategies with that objective, it generated a spirited debate among the presidential candidates.

Although the hard-line policy proposed by the CDA was supported by most Republicans and conservative Democrats, its possible negative repercussions for U.S. foreign relations troubled many who, at least in principle, supported the proposal. Among other things, the bill would prohibit trade with Cuba by U.S. subsidiaries in third countries and block access to U.S. ports for ships that had recently visited Cuban ports. Even President Bush was concerned, and refused to support the CDA on the grounds that the subsidiary provision would damage U.S. relations with important allies.[5]

The Democratic candidate, liberal Bill Clinton, also refused to support the bill. However, as the campaign intensified during the summer months, Bill Clinton surprised the political world when he declared himself in favor of the Torricelli bill. At a fund-raiser in Miami, organized by the predominantly Republican and conservative Cuban American National Foundation, Clinton justified his new position by explaining: "I think that this administration [Bush-Quayle] has missed a big opportunity to put the hammer down on Fidel Castro and Cuba."[6] Not to be outdone by his challenger, several days later President Bush also reversed himself and endorsed the CDA.

The Cuba issue served Bill Clinton well during the campaign, and although he failed to carry Florida, he managed to defeat George Bush in the November elections. Despite Clinton's position on the CDA, the Democrats' electoral victory raised the Cuban government's hopes and expectations for better relations with the United States. Cuban officials were hopeful that Bill Clinton's hardline position on the CDA was only campaign rhetoric. They expected a liberal Democrat to be an improvement over the previous twelve years of conservative Republicanism under Reagan and Bush.

As part of its overall strategy to survive after the disintegration of the Soviet Union and the signing of the Cuban Democracy Act into law in October 1992, the Cuban government aggressively pursued foreign investments and trade relations with Europe, Latin America, and Asia. At the same time, Cuba sought to establish a new dialogue with its emigre community. In April 1994, at a conference organized and hosted by Foreign Minister Roberto Robaina, the government invited 220 Cubans living in twenty-five countries for three days of talks in Havana. Although modest in scope, the talks were perceived as serious by most participants, and they concluded with the government's commitment to improve communications between itself and the emigres, to relax most travel restrictions to the island, and, most important, to hold more meetings with a wider agenda.[7]

Cuban Migration to the United States in the 1980s

Despite the crisis the Mariel boatlift created for the Carter administration and the State of Florida, the United States government continued treating Cuban immigration on a crisis-to-crisis basis—as part of a political strategy designed to overthrow the revolution, instead of a rational and humane immigration policy. The Cuban government was also guilty of playing politics with the migratory process, and treating emigration—especially the Mariel boatlift—as a domestic political issue with the objectives of eliminating political opposition and consolidating the revolution. As a result, as soon as the immediate crisis was over in the fall of 1980, both governments returned to their familiar Cold War positions and resumed their war of words. The Radio Martí issue and the

Cuban American National Foundation's lobbying efforts against the Cuban government justified Cuba's reluctance to negotiate an immigration agreement with the United States. By the same token, the Reagan administration, responding to the Republican party's most conservative constituents, was equally reluctant to negotiate with Cuba. After all, during the 1980 presidential campaign, Reagan and the Republicans had harshly criticized Carter's "soft stance on Cuba," and the way he had "mishandled" the Mariel boatlift. Under those circumstances, an agreement on immigration would have to wait until the political climate between the two nations changed, or another crisis forced the parties to negotiate.

In the absence of a working immigration agreement between the U.S. and Cuba, a rare government–private sector collaboration emerged. The Cuban American National Foundation created, and the U.S. State Department approved, the "Exodus" program, to arrange the immigration to the United States of Cubans who had managed to arrive at third countries. Using a combination of public and private funds, and working with the potential immigrants' relatives in the U.S., the Foundation—providing medical insurance and employment opportunities for one year—sponsored more than 9,500 Cubans between 1988 and 1993. It is estimated that the Foundation's Cuban Exodus Relief Fund received about $2 million in federal assistance during those years.

The program was quite successful, but it was not nearly enough to satisfy the Cubans' growing demands to emigrate. In addition, the program also raised some questions about its legality and politics. Wayne Smith, the State Department's senior representative in Havana during the Carter and Reagan administrations, told the *New York Times*:

> I do not know of any other political organization in the United States that has ever received this kind of privilege. . . . It is one [privilege] they have clearly used to their advantage, saying to people, we can get your uncle in Madrid to the U.S. and, oh, by the way, you do support the Foundation, don't you?[8]

An issue that the United States was willing and hoping to negotiate with the Cuban government was the return of more than 2,700 Mariel "excludables" in U.S. prisons. The "Marielito" stigma seemed to be getting worse, as the U.S. mass media continued making their "criminality" the focus of numerous news stories.[9]

Thus, responding to a combination of pressures from those who wanted the "criminals returned to Castro" to human rights groups who underlined the illegality of detaining individuals indefinitely without a trial, in 1987 the United States entered into negotiations with Cuba in order to settle the "excludables" issue, and to reactivate the 1984 accords (see chapter 7). Although the Cuban government saw the return of the Mariel excludables as a political defeat, it was under great pressure to reopen a legal and direct migratory channel to the United States.

The renewed agreement was welcomed by both governments, but received a violent response from those who would be most adversely affected by it: the 2,700 "excludables" who would be deported to Cuba. Ignored by the U.S. justice system as they served their endless sentences, the Cuban inmates at the federal penitentiaries of Oakdale, Louisiana, and Atlanta, Georgia, rioted and demanded individual asylum hearings. The riots left more than 200 inmates and prison officials injured, and more than $100 million in damages.[10]

The 1987 agreement merely reactivated the 1984 accords, which were expected to normalize the migratory process between the two countries. Most important among the measures taken were the continued deportation of the Mariel inmates, and the renewed U.S. promise to issue 20,000 visas a year to Cubans who qualified to immigrate. The agreement, however, was never executed as intended. The United States Interest Section in Havana, claiming to be overwhelmed by visa requests, never came close to issuing the 20,000 visas a year stipulated by the accord, a point Castro did not allow to go unnoticed. In a 1994 speech, the Cuban president accused the United States of dragging its feet and violating the spirit and letter of the agreement. With the aid of figures provided by the Cuban and U.S. Coast Guards (see table 9.1 below), he explained that from 1985 to 1994, the United States issued 11,222 visas, only 7.1 percent of the 160,000 the two governments had agreed to under the accord. Castro also explained that during the same period, the United States had admitted 13,275 Cubans who arrived in Florida illegally.[11]

Castro's arguments and reasoning were not too different from a report prepared by the U.S. Interest Section in January 1994. In a top secret memorandum to the State Department, C.I.A., and I.N.S., visa officers in the Interest Section discussed the difficulties

Table 9.1   Number of "Rafters" by year (1985–1994)

Year	Immigrant visas issued by US	Illegal rafters to US	Rafters detained by Cuba
1985	1227	—	—
1986*	—	—	—
1987*	—	—	—
1988	3472	—	—
1989	1631	—	—
1990	1098	467	1593
1991	1376	1997	6596
1993	964	4208	11564
1994	544	4092	10975
Total	11222	13275	37801

* Suspension of 1984 agreement by Cuba, in protest for the Reagan administration's creation of Radio Martí.

Source: La Razón es nuestra: Comparencia de Fidel Castro en la TV cubana y las ondas internacionales de Radio Habana Cuba. 24 de agosto de 1994. Editorial Política, La Habana, Cuba, 1994, p. 54.

they were having identifying visa applicants with legitimate human rights cases:

> The processing of refugee applicants continues to show weak cases. Most people apply more because of the deteriorating economic situation than a real fear of persecution. . . . Although we have tried hard to work with those human rights organizations on which we exert greater control to identify activists truly persecuted by the government, human rights cases represent the weakest category of the refugee program.[12]

By 1990 it was clear that the 1984/1987 immigration accords were not working to anyone's satisfaction. At the same time, the collapse of the Soviet Union and most Communist governments in Europe eliminated most of Cuba's trading partners. That, in addition to the U.S. economic embargo, low productivity, and mismanagement, sent the Cuban economy into a tailspin. The economic crisis, coupled with increased pressure and opposition from human rights groups, presented the Cuban government with one of the most potentially explosive social situations since 1959. As a result, the number of people leaving the country illegally by sea increased dramatically from 467 in 1990 to 3,656 in 1993. In 1994 the numbers increased steadily from 716 in April, to 21,300 in August.[13] The steady rise in arrivals worried many Florida officials who feared another Mariel-style boatlift from Cuba.[14]

The fast and steady increase in Cuban rafters gave rise to the "Hermanos al Rescate" (Brothers to the Rescue) organization. The group was organized in May 1991 by José Basulto and twenty-five volunteer pilots who scoured the sea between Florida and Cuba looking for rafters. The group has been very successful in spotting thousands of rafters and contributing to their rescue by informing the U.S. Coast Guard of the rafters' location.

Although Basulto is a Bay of Pigs veteran, he claims to be above politics, and insists that Brothers to the Rescue is an organization guided by strictly humanitarian motives: "We are trying to break through the partisanship that exists in Miami by communicating a message of love, understanding, and hope."[15] There is no reason to doubt Basulto's words or question his motives; on the contrary, his dedication and efforts must be praised and applauded. Nevertheless, the existence of a private rescue operation, with the approval of the U.S. government, raises important legal and political questions. Chief among these are the contradictions and unfairness of U.S. immigration policy underlined by the group. In 1991 and 1992, the first two years Brothers to the Rescue was in operation, the United States reinforced its Haitian interdiction program by deporting thousands back to Haiti and detaining more than 30,000 in Guantánamo Bay to await deportation.[16]

Brothers to the Rescue unintentionally exposed the double standard in U.S. immigration policy as applied to Cubans and Haitians. The United States could not justify encouraging and allowing the rescue of Cubans while denying Haitians the opportunity to plead their cases for asylum. The policy's unfairness became an issue during the 1992 U.S. presidential election:

> During the campaign, Clinton bitterly assailed George Bush's cruel Haitian policies, particularly his harsh treatment of refu-

gees. Clinton moved quickly to change these policies as he took office, harshening them still further by extending the (flatly illegal) blockade on Haiti to prevent refugees from escaping the mounting terror—all for humanitarian reasons; the goal was to save lives. Those who fled remained "economic refugees." Clinton's increased brutality proved to be a grand success. Refugee flow, which had reached over 30,000 in 1992, sharply declined under Clinton's ministrations, to about the level of 1989, before the decline under Aristide.[17]

The Summer of 1994: A New Cuban Migration Crisis

In scenes reminiscent of the events and incidents leading to the Mariel boatlift of 1980, a series of embassy invasions and boat hijackings by Cubans seeking asylum disturbed the usually peaceful city of Havana from May to August 1994. On May 28, more than one hundred people forcefully entered the Belgian ambassador's residence. On July 13, twenty-one people entered the German embassy. Two days later, nine people entered the Chilean consulate. The embassy crises were resolved without violence or fatalities. Most boat hijackings, however, had violent outcomes. On July 13, at least thirty-two people drowned when a hijacked tugboat was rammed by two Cuban Coast Guard tugboats in the port of Havana. On July 26 and August 3 and 4, the boat that has transported passengers from Havana to the city of Regla for nearly 100 years was hijacked to Miami. Violence was used in all these hijackings, and one on August 4 resulted in the death of a Cuban police officer.[18]

On August 5, as these incidents became more frequent and violent, President Castro held a televised news conference to explain the Cuban government's position. Castro was visibly angry, not with his national television audience, but with the U.S. government. Earlier that day, Cuban police had put down a small riot in the city of Havana. The riot, Castro claimed, was caused by rumors of a "United States-sponsored boatlift to Miami." He went on to say that if the United States continued encouraging illegal migration, the government of Cuba would discontinue its policy of stopping people trying to emigrate illegally:

Either they [the United States] take serious measures to guard their coasts, or we will stop putting obstacles in the way of people who want to leave the country, and we will stop putting obstacles in the way of people [in the United States] who want to come and look for their relatives here.[19]

Castro's words were not unfamiliar to his audience. He had used similar language in 1965 when he announced the boatlift from the port of Camarioca (see chapter 5), and again in 1980 to announce the Mariel boatlift (see chapter 6). Even more portentous, however, was the fact that like during the previous boatlifts, Cuba was experiencing a period of economic hardships and crisis. The big difference was that, unlike 1965 and 1980, the 1994 economic crisis was the worst in the revolution's history. The economy seemed to have hit bottom, and as consumer goods, food, and petroleum supplies became more scarce, the people became increasingly tense and restless.

News of the August 5 riot in Havana appeared in most major newspapers in the United States, but the news was bigger and more ominous in Miami, where many analysts saw the incident as the beginning of the end for Castro. Many Cuban American political activists were convinced that Castro would not be able to survive the usually fatal combination of economic crisis and popular discontent.[20]

The riot clearly added to the Cuban government's problems, and as the economic crisis worsened in 1994, the number of Cubans arriving in the coasts of Florida in home-made and extremely unsafe "balsas" (rafts) reached alarming proportions. Thousands of Cubans concluded that the economy would not improve anytime soon, and decided to emigrate by whatever means possible. Ernesto Rodríguez Chávez, a Cuban analyst who has studied the factors influencing Cuban emigration, argues that in addition to Cuba's economic crisis, rafters were also driven by the historical guarantee that they would be welcomed by the U.S. government— "a welcome that had been specially warm for those arriving in July and August, 1994, after stealing boats, using violence, endangering the lives of people who did not wish to emigrate, and even committing murder. Rafters were further reassured and encouraged by the U.S. government's pledge not to change its immigration policy toward Cubans under any circumstances."[21]

The United States responded to Cuba's economic and political crises with clear signs of encouragement for those who tried to escape from the island. Indeed, so many tried that August 1994 soon became a record-setting month in the history of the Cuban migration to the United States, a fact that captured the attention of the U.S. mass media. The *New York Times*, the *Miami Herald*, *El Nuevo Herald*, *Time*, and *Newsweek* were among the many newspapers and magazines that tried to keep up with the record-setting numbers by publishing daily or weekly tables and graphs.[22] It was estimated that at least 25,000 "balseros" (rafters), travelling on anything that floated, had headed north from the port town of Cojímar, Cuba, during the month. The migration from Cuba was back on the front pages, and the headlines were as dramatic as ever: "U.S. Coast Guard to Guard Florida Straits";[23] "Vessels Prepared to Head off any Exodus from Cuba";[24] "We Won't Allow Another Mariel";[25] "U.S. Hints at Blockade."[26] As in the past, the United States seemed to have been caught by surprise, and was again reacting to a Cuban immigration crisis with little control over the events.

The United States government's lack of control over the migration, and the high number of daily arrivals, prompted some analysts to compare the August exodus with the Mariel boatlift of 1980, and the comparison was not without merit. For example, it was clear that Castro could control the migration at will. In three televised addresses to the Cuban people—one carried live by CNN in the United States—Castro repeatedly explained that because of the long history of U.S. encouragement for Cubans to leave the country illegally, and in light of the recent series of hijackings of state-owned vessels, his government would stop putting obstacles in the way of people wishing to leave the country.[27]

At least three factors, however, made the new crisis different from the Mariel boatlift: 1) The numbers had the potential to be higher in 1994 than in 1980. On August 23, the U.S. Coast Guard rescued a single-day record of 2,886 Cubans in the Florida Straits. And in the twelve-day period of August 13 to 25, the Coast Guard rescued 13,084 rafters, a much larger number than the 9,340 who arrived during the first twelve days of Mariel. The total number of rescues for the month of August was 21,300.[28] 2) Unlike Jimmy Carter's inability to stop the Mariel boatlift during its early days, Bill Clinton announced on August 19 that Cubans would not be allowed to enter United States territory. Instead, they would be rescued at sea and detained, indefinitely, by U.S. naval authorities.[29] 3) Also unlike Jimmy Carter's reluctance and failure to negotiate

Table 9.2   Coast Guard Cuban Rescue Statistics

Year	Number of People Rescued	% Increase over Previous Year
1981	n/a	—
1982	n/a	—
1983	47	—
1984	19	− 60
1985	43	+ 56
1986	27	− 37
1987	44	+ 63
1988	59	+ 34
1989	391	+ 563
1990	467	+ 19
1991	2,203	+ 372
1992	2,557	+ 16
1993	3,656	+ 43
1994	37,139	+ 916

Source: Seventh Coast Guard Public Affairs Office, Miami

Quoted here from: Max J. Castro. "Cuba: The Continuing Crisis." *The North South Agenda.* No. 13, April, 1995, p. 4.

with Castro, the Clinton administration was able to negotiate an agreement with the Cuban government to stop the exodus.

Bill Clinton was determined to prevent another Mariel. When the governor of Florida declared a state emergency, the president consulted with the governor, Jorge Más Canosa of the Cuban American National Foundation, and other Florida political and civic leaders. On August 19, President Clinton announced that Cuban rafters would no longer be transported to the United States. They would instead be detained indefinitely in the U.S. naval base at Guantánamo. The next day the president announced that in addition to detaining the rafters, the U.S. government would take the following measures: 1) visits to Cuba by Cuban Americans were to be restricted, except on extreme humanitarian cases; 2) Cuban Americans were no longer allowed to send money remittances to their relatives in Cuba; and 3) a special U.S. Treasury Department license was now required for journalists and academics wishing to travel to Cuba.[30]

The president's orders to stop the Cuban rafters represented a complete reversal of a thirty-five-year-old immigration policy designed to welcome as political refugees almost any Cuban who claimed to be "escaping" Fidel Castro's repression. Cubans, to whom the doors to the United States had been open since 1959, were suddenly not only denied entry to the United States, but were being intercepted at sea and taken to what they came to call "concentration camps" at the U.S. military base at Guantánamo Bay. Once on the base they were technically in a safe haven, out of danger, and without the right to claim political asylum in the United States. U.S. Attorney General Janet Reno emphatically announced that the more than 20,000 Cuban rafters at Guantánamo would be held there indefinitely, and would "not be processed for admission to the United States."[31]

The change in policy came as a shock to Cubans, who had come to believe that immigrating to the United States was a natural right. Still, the announcement did not deter the flow of rafters right away. On the contrary, the days following Clinton's orders set new one-day records. On August 22, the U.S. Coast Guard picked up 2,338 rafters, and 2,886 more on August 23.[32]

To show its resolve, the administration, in an unprecedented move, asked the Cuban government to dissuade rafters from leaving Cuba. Cuba's agreement to use only "peaceful persuasion," coupled with Washington's threat of "indefinite detention," dashed the hopes of the would-be refugees. For the first time in thirty-five years, the United States was refusing to allow immigration from Cuba. It was also the first time in thirty-five years that the U.S. and Cuban governments had joined forces to stop refugees fleeing from a country categorized as a serious human rights violator by the U.S. Department of State.

The U.S.–Cuba collaboration gradually ended the exodus, and on September 1, 1994, the United States and Cuba initiated a round of conversations on immigration issues affecting both countries. Cuba proposed a wider agenda to discuss all issues preventing the two countries from having normal diplomatic relations—in particular, the thirty-two-year-old U.S. economic embargo against Cuba. The Clinton administration insisted on discussing immigration issues only, and Castro conceded.

The first round of talks was held in New York City and concluded on September 10, with the Cuban government's promise to continue its policy of peacefully dissuading potential migrants from taking to sea on unsafe vessels, and to allow any detained rafters wishing to return to Cuba to do so without fear of reprisals. In return, the U.S. government agreed to accept 20,000 Cuban immigrants each year, and to persuade all detained rafters to return to Cuba to apply for visas to the United States.[33]

The 28,000 rafters in U.S. custody reacted with anger and violence to the U.S.–Cuba negotiations. Some 2,500 Guantánamo detainees rioted, injuring more than 200 U.S. soldiers, and more than 100 escaped from the detention camps in Panama. They felt betrayed and confused by the new position of the U.S. Nevertheless, despite the Clinton administration's hard-line rhetoric of "indefinite detention," most rafters—and their relatives in Miami—were optimistic that sooner or later they would be allowed to immigrate to the United States.

May 2, 1995: End of the Open-Door Policy?

The Clinton administration's policy of indefinite detention received harsh criticism from the powerful Cuban American community in Miami, human rights organizations, some Latin American governments, and the rafters themselves. The pressure led to a gradual softening of the policy. In October 1994, the U.S. Attorney General announced that while most rafters were destined to remain indefinitely at Guantánamo as planned, those seventy years old or older, the critically or chronically ill, pregnant women, and minors with their parents, would be allowed to immigrate to the United States. This change, along with the nearly 1,000 rafters who had voluntarily returned to Cuba, gradually reduced the detainee population by almost 20 percent, but the U.S. would still have to find a way of settling another 21,000 Cubans.

The policy revision was the first indication of the administration's attempts to find a way out of a policy that in addition to being unpopular and controversial was also extremely expensive. Start-up costs for the Guantánamo tent city were estimated at $100 million. Another $35 million were invested in improvements to the base infrastructure in order to accommodate the long-term population. Finally, the daily operations cost $1 million per day. Based on operating costs alone—at least $365 million a year—it was very unlikely that the administration could keep the Guantánamo operation going for a long time.

In addition to the high costs of the Guantánamo operation, there was also the fear of more rioting and violence due to the deplorable living conditions in the camps. In April 1995, the Pentagon issued a report that reflected those fears, and recommended closing the camps as soon as possible. Despite a significant increase in military personnel at the base, the summer months were still expected to bring unrest and possibly more violence among the rafters.

On May 2, 1995, the Clinton administration relieved the military's anxieties when it announced that, after secret negotiations with the Cuban government, the two nations had reached a mutually beneficial immigration agreement. The new agreement eliminated the indefinite detention provision in effect since August 1994, news that brought cheers from the detained rafters and their relatives in Miami. All detainees would now be gradually admitted to the U.S. until Guantánamo was emptied of rafters sometime in March 1996. The agreement, however, also called for the direct deportation of any rafter attempting to enter the U.S. illegally.

As could be expected, reaction to the Cuba–U.S. agreement on deportation was mixed and emotional. The U.S. government believed it was the best solution for a bad situation. The United States could not continue holding people indefinitely, nor could it afford to take in unlimited numbers of refugees. The agreement set a generous immigration quota for Cubans—a minimum of 20,000 per year—and established an orderly immigration procedure in Cuba that guaranteed the safety of deportees and new applicants. The Cuban government hailed the agreement as sound. In particular, Ricardo Alarcón was pleased because the accords eliminated the Cubans' "exclusivity," a weapon the U.S. had used against Cuba since 1959: "from this moment on, Cubans will be treated the same way as people of other nationalities."[34] But the Cuban American community in the United States saw the new agreement as U.S. treason against the cause of Cuban liberation.

On May 9, 1995, exactly a week after the agreement, an unprecedented, and until the previous week unthinkable, event took place in the small Cuban port town of Cabañas. A U.S. Coast Guard cutter docked at the port and surrendered 13 Cuban rafters to Cuban immigration officers. On the dock, representatives of the U.S.

Interest Section in Havana greeted the deportees and offered them guidance on how to apply for U.S. visas.

The arrival in Cuba of the first deported rafters proved that the new immigration accords were working, and that the U.S. and Cuba were capable of reaching agreements and working together when the interests of both countries were at stake. Yet despite the rare show of cooperation, the United States still refuses to recognize the Cuban government, continues its economic embargo against the island, and keeps in effect the travel restrictions imposed by Clinton in 1994.

Notes

1. The collapse of the Soviet Union and the end of Communism led many—especially in the Cuban American community—to believe that Castro's days were numbered. The expectations were so high that in 1990, the *Miami Herald* held a contest for readers to predict Castro's final days. The winning contestant would be awarded an all-expenses-paid vacation in Cuba's famous resort at Varadero Beach. The contest was suspended two years later without a winner. An equally speculative and presumptuous book was Andrés Oppenheimer's *Castro's Final Hour: The Secret Story behind the Coming Downfall of Communist Cuba* (New York, 1992). For serious academic analysis on U.S.–Cuba relations after the Cold War, see Guillian Gunn, *Cuba in Transition: Options for U.S. Policy* (New York, 1993); Enrique Baloyra and James Morris, eds., *Conflict and Change in Cuba* (Albuquerque, 1993); Carollee Bengelsdorf, *The Problem of Democracy in Cuba* (New York, 1994); and Sandor Halebsky and John Kirk, eds., *Cuba in Transition: Crisis and Transformation* (Boulder, 1992).

2. For more detailed accounts and analysis of the peace process in Central America, see James Dunkerley, *The Pacification of Central America* (London, 1994); United Nations, *Acuerdos de el Salvador: en el camino de la paz* (New York, 1992).

3. Unable to predict how long the Nicaraguan Revolution would last, the I.N.S. was reluctant to apply the open arms policy to Nicaraguans who, like the Cubans, were fleeing what the U.S. Government labeled a "Marxist" regime. In the absence of a clear policy, many Nicaraguans were deported and others were kept in a state of constant uncertainty. The case of Julio Justo Somarriba provides a good illustration of the highly politicized and incoherent policy. Mr. Somarriba was a teacher who fled Nicaragua after losing his job for "refusing to indoctrinate his students in Sandinista and Communist propaganda." He entered the U.S. illegally through Mexico, and applied for political asylum. His claim was denied twice, on the grounds that it was "frivolous." Fortunately for Mr. Somarriba, a few days before his scheduled deportation he won $5.5 million dollars in the Florida Lottery. The I.N.S. offered to hear the case again, and granted the new millionaire political asylum within 48 hours. See the *New York Times*, May 4, 1989, 1.

4. For a thorough discussion of the political and refugee situation in Haiti, see James Ridgeway, *The Haiti Files* (Washington, D.C., 1994); NACLA Editors, *Haiti: Dangerous Crossroads* (Boston, 1995); Brenda Gayle Plummer, *Haiti and the United States* (London, 1992); Paul Farmer, *The Uses of Haiti* (Monroe, Maine,

1994); Ronald Fernández, *Cruising the Caribbean* (Monroe, Maine, 1994); Maryse Fontus, Laura Sherman, and Arthur Helton, *Refugee Refoulement* (New York, 1990).

5. Gunn, *Cuba in Transition*, 20–26.

6. Ibid., 21.

7. The three days of talks between the Cuban government and Cuban exiles caused quite a stir in Miami, where participants were accused of treason in the local press and some were threatened with physical violence. For more on the Cuban American community's reaction to the conference, see the *Miami Herald* and *El Nuevo Herald*, April 20–30, 1994; *Contrapunto*, (May 1994, June 1994); Human Rights Watch, "Dangerous Dialogue Revisited: Threats to Freedom of Expression Continue in Miami's Cuban Exile Community," (November 1994). The conference's proceedings were published in Cuba by Editora Política, *La nación y la emigración* (Havana, 1994). The second conference has been scheduled to take place in Havana from November 3 to 6, 1995.

8. *New York Times*, May 8, 1995, 10a.

9. For more on the mass media's increased interest on the "Marielitos' " criminality, see Félix Masud-Piloto, "Changing Public Opinion Toward Mariel Entrants: The Evolution of the 'Marielito' Stigma," unpublished, presented at the Latin American Studies Association 28th Congress, Atlanta, Ga. (March 1994).

10. *Miami Herald*, December 3, 1997, 1a.

11. Fidel Castro, *La razón es nuestra* (Havana, 1994).

12. *Juventud Rebelde*, March 6, 1994, 1.

13. *Miami Herald*, August 26, 1994, 21a; January 9, 1995, 1b.

14. Executive Office of the Governor, "The Unfair Burden: Immigration's Impact on Florida" (March, 1994). The federal government also developed a confidential emergency plan called "Operation Distant Shore" in anticipation of a Mariel-style exodus. *Miami Herald*, August 18, 1994, 1a.

15. *Miami Herald*, July 5, 1992, 1b.

16. For a good discussion on the Haitian interdiction program and the living conditions for Haitians at Guantánamo, see Paul Farmer, *The Uses of Haiti* (Monroe, Maine, 1994), 225–296.

17. Noam Chomsky in the introduction to Farmer's *The Uses of Haiti* (Monroe, Maine, 1994), 37–38.

18. Ernesto Rodríguez Chávez, "La crisis migratoria," 14. For more details about the hijackings and their impact on Cuba and the U.S., see *El Nuevo Herald*, July 14 to August 10, 1994.

19. *Miami Herald*, August 6, 1994, 1a.

20. *El Nuevo Herald*, August 6, 1994, 1b.

21. Rodríguez Chávez, Ibid., 15.

22. In addition to the extensive coverage on the rafters and the record numbers, the popular press produced some interesting pieces. One of the most noteworthy things was the change in language used by the press. For example, *Time* magazine had a cover article titled "Cubans Go Home," hostile words never before used in reference to the Cuban migration. *Time*, September 5, 1994, 29–38. For daily statistics on the rafters, see the *Miami Herald* and *El Nuevo Herald*, July 1 to September 30, 1994.

23. *Miami Herald*, August 11, 1994, 1a.

24. Ibid.

25. Ibid., August 19, 1994, 1a.

26. Ibid., August 22, 1994, 1a.

27. Castro, "La Razon," 33.

28. *New York Times*, September 9, 1994.

29. *Miami Herald*, August 20, 1994, 1a.

30. *Miami Herald*, August 21, 1994, 1a.

31. Ibid., 1a.

32. Ibid., August 24, 1994, 1a.

33. For details on the agreement, see *New York Times* and *Miami Herald*, September 11, 1994, 1a.

34. *Miami Herald*, May 3, 1995, 1a.

Conclusions

BACK IN THE NINETEENTH CENTURY, when Cuban nationalists were trying to liberate their country from the Spanish empire, they looked to the United States for philosophical guidance, material aid and, at times, a haven from repression and persecution. Thus, from the 1860s on, a Cuban presence existed in the United States, especially in Florida. After the struggle for independence, however, the United States came to dominate Cuba's politics and economy to the extent of turning the island into an American protectorate, if not a colony.

Using military force on several occasions and manipulative diplomacy in others, the United States interfered in every Cuban government from Tomás Estrada Palma's to Fulgencio Batista's. Aided and abetted by a dependent class of Cuban politicians, this relationship helped nurture strong nationalist and at times anti–United States passions which, once unleashed, would be hard to control. Fidel Castro's revolution in 1959 gave expression to those passions and to aspirations for fundamental change in Cuba.

Castro's movement thus took on a radical character, which many Cubans and the U.S. government opposed and which led to the migration of more than one million Cubans to the United States between 1959 and 1995. The migration was at first predominantly political, although its motives changed later. But whatever the motives, the U.S. government consistently depicted post-1959 Cuban migrants as political refugees escaping "Communist terror."

Many Cuban exiles, especially those who left between 1959 and 1962, were undoubtedly escaping political persecution, and they certainly deserved political asylum. On the other hand, the United States had its own political motives for accepting as many refugees from the revolution as possible. Unlike all pre-1959 Cuban governments, the revolutionary leadership refused to be dominated by the United States, and it posed a serious threat to U.S. economic and strategic interests, thus attracting the ire of successive U.S. administrations.

In response to the revolutionary government's "defiance," President Eisenhower initiated an unwritten open-door policy for Cuban refugees to weaken and discredit Castro and the revolution. The strategy was expected to cause a crippling "brain drain" and an embarrassing mass exodus. With a leftist revolution that was widely admired throughout Latin America, it was feared that Cuba would undermine the U.S. Cold War "sphere of influence." The policy worked in the short run by denying Cuba many of its best-trained minds. Ironically, the policy also worked to Cuba's long-run advantage by eliminating the most disaffected sectors of the old order and allowing the revolution a quicker and smoother consolidation of power.

Eisenhower's actions were affected by several factors. First, the Cold War, which had allegedly spread to the Western Hemisphere via Guatemala in the early 1950s, tended to confuse local movements for social change with superpower manipulations on their global chessboard. Second, "communism" was a potent and highly emotional issue in U.S. domestic policies, as McCarthyism, the "who lost China" controversy, and the Nixon–Kennedy debates of 1960 showed. Until the late 1970s, no U.S. president could take a conciliatory stance toward Cuba, and even President Carter's modest rapprochement with Cuba attracted a storm of opposition. Third, the Cuban revolution rapidly demonstrated that it posed a serious economic and strategic threat to traditional U.S. interests, not only in the island itself but perhaps throughout Latin America. Fourth, the open-door refugee policy was only part of a U.S. effort to destroy the Cuban revolution. Also planned were political assassinations and economic sabotage, as well as the use of exiles in military operations against the revolutionary regime. Fifth, a genuine humanitarian concern existed in the United States for those who feared persecution or execution by the revolutionary government.

From its inception, then, the Cuban Refugee Program was marked by multiple and sometimes contradictory elements. For example, mixing Cold War ideology with humanitarian refugee concerns would lead to future problems with refugees from non-Communist nations allied to the United States. Attempting to control the political process in Cuba, the United States sacrificed some control over its own borders, which became a major controversy by the 1980s. Moreover, the refugee program may actually have helped consolidate the revolutionary government in Cuba.

As long as commercial flights operated between Havana and Miami, Eisenhower's open-door policy worked mostly to the United States' advantage. The brain drain continued its steady flow, and the American press provided extensive coverage and dramatic headlines about the exodus from Communist Cuba. With the cancellation of regular flights in 1962, however, Cubans wishing to emigrate to the United States had to go through a third country and comply with a lengthy and expensive procedure to obtain U.S. entry permits.

By the mid-1960s, the political motive of the Cuban migration declined. Thereafter, most Cubans who left the country did so for economic reasons or to reunify families. In the absence of regular migratory channels between the United States and Cuba, and to defuse potentially serious internal discontent, the Cuban government decided to allow exiled Cubans to pick up relatives at the port of Camarioca in 1965, and at the port of Mariel in 1980. The two boatlifts and the airlift between 1965 and 1973 ultimately brought 400,000 Cubans to the United States.

From January 1959 to August 1994, Cuban migrants received special treatment from the U.S. government, which bent the law or created new statutes to keep up with the influx. United States taxpayers paid over $2 billion for the Cuban Refugee Program to help the emigres resettle in the United States. Such treatment underlined a glaring inconsistency in the 1980s as the United States faced multiple refugee influxes from Haiti, El Salvador, Nicaragua, Guatemala, and other Caribbean Basin nations. Unlike the Cubans, who were welcomed as heroes, Haitians and Central American refugees were detained upon their arrival in the United States and arbitrarily deported to their home countries to face repression, persecution, and often execution.

For more than thirty-five years, stimulated by the Cuban refugee phenomenon, the United States used a political test rooted in Cold War ideology to grant or deny refugee status to immigrants. Those escaping the repression of left-wing governments opposed by the U.S. were invariably welcomed, while those escaping the repression of right-wing governments supported by the U.S. were systematically rejected. Chronic economic suffering throughout Latin America and the Caribbean has stimulated migration and intensified the human pressure on U.S. borders, raising the issue of whether it is possible—as the U.S. government maintains—to separate politics from economics as motives for migration and the resulting humanitarian concerns for migrants. "Controlling our borders" has become a controversial and emotional issue in U.S. politics, but conflicting interest groups and contradictory attitudes about immigrants make the formulation of a rational, humane immigration policy an elusive quest. The Sanctuary Movement of the 1980s added a moral tone and fervor reminiscent of the abolitionists and civil rights advocates of the past, but had a limited impact on policy. Thousands of Central Americans were still deported to their native countries and many were killed.

Cubans, Haitians, Central Americans, and others from the region will continue to seek entry to the United States as long as justice and their basic human needs, rights, and dignity are denied them in their native lands. It is impossible to predict how and when these migration flows will take place, or if there will be another Cuban boatlift, or if Haitians will again take to the sea to escape renewed political unrest in Haiti. Contradictions, uncertainty, discrimination, and even prison have faced most refugees in the past, while others have enjoyed a welcoming open door. Those who seek refuge now and in the future deserve to know what to expect. It is time for the United States to adopt a single, nonideological, humanitarian standard for granting refugee status.

Bibliography

Manuscripts

Dwight D. Eisenhower Papers. Dwight D. Eisenhower Library, Abilene, Kansas.

Christian Herter Papers. Dwight D. Eisenhower Library, Abilene, Kansas.

Lyndon B. Johnson Papers. Lyndon B. Johnson Library, Austin, Texas.

John F. Kennedy Papers. John F. Kennedy Library, Boston, Massachusetts.

Robert E. Merriam Papers. Dwight D. Eisenhower Library, Abilene, Kansas.

Arthur M. Schlesinger, Jr., Papers. John F. Kennedy Library, Boston, Massachusetts.

Theodore C. Sorensen Papers. John F. Kennedy Library, Boston, Massachusetts.

Government Documents

Government of Cuba. *Jamás nos rendiremos*. Editora Política, 1980.

———. *Una batalla por nuestra soberanía*. Havana: Editora Política, 1980.

Prohías, Rafael J., and Lourdes Casal. "The Cuban Minority in the United States: Preliminary Report on Need Identification and Program Evaluation." Washington, D.C.: U.S. Government Printing Office (hereafter GPO), 1974.

Public Papers of the Presidents of the United States. Jimmy Carter. Washington, D.C.: GPO, 1977–1961.

———. Dwight D. Eisenhower. Washington, D.C.: GPO, 1953–1961.

———. Lyndon B. Johnson. Washington, D.C.: GPO, 1964–1969.

———. John F. Kennedy. Washington, D.C.: GPO, 1962–1964.

———. Richard M. Nixon. Washington, D.C.: GPO, 1969–1974.

U.S. Congress. House of Representatives, Committee on the Judiciary. Subcommittee on Immigration, Citizenship, and International Law. *Hearings on Haitian Emigration*, 94th Cong., 2d sess., 1976.

———. *Hearings on the Caribbean Refugee Crisis: Cubans and Haitians*. 96th Cong., 2d sess., 1980.

———. Staff Report. Subcommittee on Oversight, Permanent Select Committee on Intelligence. *The Cuban Emigres: Was There a U.S. Intelligence Failure?* Washington, D.C.: GPO, 1980.

U.S. Congress. Senate, Committee on the Judiciary. *Hearings on Cuban Refugee Problems*. 87th Cong., 2d sess., 1961.

———. *Cuban Refugee Problems: Hearings Before the Subcommittee to Investigate Problems Connected with Refugees and Escapees*. 7th Cong., 1st sess., 1962.

———. Select Committee to Study Governmental Operations with Respect to

Intelligence Activity. *Alleged Assassination Plots Involving Foreign Leaders*. Senate report 465, 94th Cong., 2d sess., 1975.

Books

Aguilar, Luis E. *Cuba 1933: Prologue to Revolution*. New York: Norton, 1972.
Alexander, Charles C. *Holding the Line: The Eisenhower Era, 1952–1961*. Bloomington: Indiana University Press, 1975.
Allison, Graham T. *Essence of Decision: Explaining the Cuban Missile Crisis*. Boston: Little, Brown, 1971.
Arévalo, Juan José. *The Shark and the Sardines*. New York: Lyle Stuart, 1961.
Armstrong, Robert, and Janet Schenk. *El Salvador: The Face of Revolution*. Boston: South End Press, 1982.
Ayers, Bradley Earl. *The War That Never Was: An Insider's Account of C.I.A. Covert Operations Against Cuba*. Indianapolis: Bobbs-Merrill, 1976.
Baloyra, Enrique, and James A. Morris, eds. *Conflict and Change in Cuba*. Albuquerque: University of New Mexico Press, 1993.
Bender, Lynn Darrell. *The Politics of Hostility: Castro's Revolution and United States Policy*. Hato Rey, Puerto Rico: Inter-American University Press, 1975.
Bengelsdorf, Carollee. *The Problem of Democracy in Cuba: Between Vision & Reality*. New York: Oxford University Press, 1994.
Benjamin, Medea, Joseph Collins, and Michael Scoll. *No Free Lunch: Food and Revolution in Cuba Today*. San Francisco: Institute for Food and Development Policy, 1984.
Betancourt, Luis Adrián. *Por qué Carlos?* Havana: Editorial Letras Cubanas, 1981.
Black, George, Milton Jamil, and Norma Chinchilla. *Garrison Guatemala*. New York: Monthly Review Press, 1984.
Blanco, Juan Antonio and Medea Benjamin. *Cuba: Talking About Revolution*. Melbourne, Australia: Ocean Press, 1994.
Blasier, Cole. *The Giant's Rival. The U.S.S.R. and Latin America*. Pittsburgh: University of Pittsburgh Press, 1983.
———. *The Hovering Giant: U.S. Responses to Revolutionary Changes in Latin America*. Pittsburgh: University of Pittsburgh Press, 1976.
Bonachea, Ramón L., and Marta San Martín. *The Cuban Insurrection: 1952–1959*. New Bruswick: Transaction Books, 1974.
Bonachea, Rolando E., and Nelson P. Valdés, eds. *Cuba in Revolution*. New York, Anchor Books, 1972.
Bonner, Richard. *Weakness and Deceit: U.S. Policy in El Salvador*. New York: Times Books, 1984.
Bonsal, Philip W. *Cuba, Castro and the United States*. Pittsburgh: University of Pittsburgh Press, 1971.
Booth, John A. *The End and the Beginning: The Nicaraguan Revolution*. Boulder: Westview Press, 1982.
Boswell, Thomas D., and James R. Curtis. *The Cuban-American Experience:*

Culture, Images, and Perspectives. Totowa, N.J.: Rowman & Allanheld, 1983.

Bryce-Laporte, Roy S., and Delores Mortimer, eds. *Caribbean Immigration to The United States.* Washington, D.C.: Smithsonian Institution, 1976.

Carter, Jimmy. *Keeping the Faith: Memoirs of a President.* New York: Bantam Books, 1982.

Castellanos, Gerardo. *Motivos de Cayo Hueso: contribución a la historia de la emigración revolucionaria cubana en los Estados Unidos.* Havana, 1935.

Castro, Fidel. *Informe al primer congreso del Partido Comunista de Cuba.* Havana: Editora Política, 1976.

———. *La historia me absolverá.* Barcelona: Jucas, 1976.

———. Televised speech, "La razón es nuestra," Havana: Editora Política, 1994.

Castro, Max. "Cuba: The Continuing Crisis." *The North-South Agenda* 13 (April 1995).

Chayes, Abram. *The Cuban Missile Crisis: International Crisis and the Role of Law.* New York: Oxford University Press, 1974.

Commission Pro-Justice Mariel Prisoners, ed. *Mariel Injustice.* Coral Gables, 1987.

Crassweller, Robert D. *Cuba and the U.S.: the Tangled Relationship.* New York: Foreign Policy Association, 1971.

del Pino, Rafael. *Amanecer en Girón.* Havana: Instituto Cubano del Libro, 1969.

Díaz, Ana Leonor. "Conversaciones migratorias: el bloqueo, pieza clave." *Correo de Cuba.* Vol. 1, No. 1: 38–40.

Díaz, Jesus. *De la patria y el exilio.* Havana: Unión de Escritores y Artistas de Cuba, 1979.

Diederich, Bernard. *Papa Doc: The Truth About Haiti Today.* New York: McGraw-Hill, 1969.

Dixon, Marlene, ed. *On Trial. Reagan's War Against Nicaragua: Testimony of the Permanent People's Tribunal.* San Francisco: Synthesis Publications, 1985.

Domínguez, Jorge I. *Cuba: Order and Revolution.* Cambridge, Mass.: Belknap Press, 1978.

Domínguez, Virginia R. *From Neighbor to Stranger: The Dilemma of Caribbean Peoples in the United States.* New Haven: Yale University Press, 1975.

Draper, Theodore. *Castro's Revolution: Myths and Realities.* New York: Praeger, 1962.

———. *Castroism: Theory and Practice.* New York: Praeger, 1965.

Dunkerley, James. *The Pacification of Central America: Political Change in the Isthmus, 1987–1993.* London: Verso, 1994.

Editora Política. *Conferencia: La nación y la emigración.* Havana: Editora Política, 1994.

———. *Diálogo del gobierno cubano y personas representativas de la comunidad cubana en el exterior, 1978.* Havana: Editora Política, 1994.

Eisenhower, Dwight D. *Waging Peace: White House Years, 1956–1961.* New York: Doubleday, 1965.

Fagen, Richard R., Richard Brody, and Thomas O'Leary. *Cubans in Exile: Disaffection and the Revolution.* Stanford: Stanford University Press, 1968.

Fairlie, Henry. *The Kennedy Promise: The Politics of Expectation.* Garden City: Doubleday, 1973.

Farmer, Paul. *The Uses of Haiti.* Monroe, Maine: Common Courage Press, 1994.

Fernandez, Ronald. *Cruising the Caribbean: U.S. Influence and Intervention in the Twentieth Century.* Monroe, Maine: Common Courage Press, 1994.

Fitzgibbon, Russell. *Cuba and the United States, 1900–1935.* Milwaukee: George Banta, 1935.

Foner, Philip S. *A History of Cuba and its Relations with the United States.* 2 Vols. New York: International Publishers, 1962.

————. ed. *Inside the Monster: Writings on the United States and American Imperialism by José Martí.* Translated by Eleanor Randall. New York: Monthly Review Press, 1975.

————. *The Spanish-Cuban-American War and the Birth of American Imperialism.* 2 Vols. New York: Monthly Review Press, 1972.

Fontana, Josep, ed. *José Martí: Nuestra América.* Barcelona: Editorial Ariel, 1970.

Fontus, Maryse, Laura B. Sherman, and Arthur Helton. *Refugee Refoulement: The Forced Return of Haitians Under the U.S.–Haitian Interdiction Agreement.* New York: Lawyers Committee for Human Rights, 1990.

Frank, Marc. *Cuba Looks to the Year 2000.* New York: International Publishers, 1993.

Franqui, Carlos. *Diario de la revolución.* Barcelona: Editorial Torres, 1976.

García, Angel, and Priotr Mironchick. *Esbozo histórico de las relaciones entre Cuba-Rusia, Cuba-U.R.S.S.* Havana: Editorial Ciencias Sociales, 1976.

Gellman, Irwin F. *Roosevelt and Batista: Good Neighbor Diplomacy in Cuba, 1933–1945.* Albuquerque: University of New Mexico Press, 1973.

Gil, Federico G. *Latin American-United States Relations.* New York: Harcourt Brace Jovanovich, 1971.

Gilly, Adolfo. *La nueva Nicaragua: anti-imperialismo y lucha de clases.* Mexico: Editorial Nueva Imagen, 1980.

Golden, Renny, and Michael McConnell. *Sanctuary: The New Underground Railroad.* New York: Orbis Books, 1986.

González, Edward. *Cuba Under Castro: The Limits of Charisma.* Boston: Houghton Mifflin, 1974.

Goodsell, Nelson., ed. *Fidel Castro's Personal Revolution in Cuba: 1959–1973.* New York: Knopf, 1975.

Grupo Areíto, ed. *Contra viento y marea.* Havana: René Meneses, 1978.

Gunn, Gillian. *Cuba in Transition: Options for U.S. Policy.* New York: Twentieth Century Press, 1993.

Halebsky, Sandor, and John M. Kirk, eds. *Cuba in Transition: Crisis and Transformation.* Boulder: Westview Press, 1992.

Hatchwell, Emily, and Simon Calder. *Cuba in Focus: A Guide to the People, Politics and Culture.* London: Latin American Bureau, 1995.

Heinl, Robert Debs. *Written in Blood: the Story of the Haitian People, 1492–1971*. Boston: Houghton Mifflin, 1978.

Herrera, Alicia. *Pusimos la bomba . . . y qué?*. Havana: Editorial Ciencias Sociales, 1981.

Hinckle, Warren. *The Fish Is Red: The Story of the Secret War Against Castro*. New York: Harper & Row, 1981.

Horowitz, Irving Louis. *Cuban Communism*. New Brunswick: Transaction Books, 1977.

Hunt, Howard E. *Give Us This Day*. New Rochelle: Arlington House, 1973.

Immerman, Richard H. *The C.I.A. in Guatemala*. Austin: University of Texas Press, 1982.

James, Daniel. *Cuba: The First Soviet Satellite in the Americas*. New York: Avon Books, 1961.

Janis, Irving L. *Victims of Group Think: A Psychological Study of Foreign Policy Decisions and Fiascos*. Boston: Houghton Mifflin, 1972.

Jaszi, Oscar. *Revolution and Counter-revolution in Hungary*. New York: Howard Fertig, 1969.

Jezer, Mary. *The Dark Ages: Life in the United States, 1945–1960*. Boston: South End Press, 1982.

Johnson, Haynes. *The Bay of Pigs: The Leaders' Story of Brigade 2506*. New York: Norton, 1964.

Jonas, Susanne, Ed McCaughon, and Elizabeth Sutherland Martínez, eds. *Guatemala: Tyranny on Trial. Testimony of the Permanent People's Tribunal*. San Francisco: Synthesis Publications, 1984.

Karol, K. S. *Guerrillas in Power: The Course of the Cuban Revolution*. Translated by Arnold Pomerans. New York: Hill & Wang, 1970.

Kennedy, Robert F. *Thirteen Days: A Memoir of the Cuban Missile Crisis*. New York: Norton, 1969.

Kiraly, Dela K., and Paul Jonas, eds. *The Hungarian Revolution of 1956 in Retrospect*. New York: Columbia University Press, 1978.

Kirk, John M. *José Martí: Mentor of the Cuban Nation*. Tampa: University of South Florida Press, 1983.

La Feber, Walter. *America, Russia, and the Cold War, 1945–1980*. New York: Wiley, 1980.

————. *Inevitable Revolutions: The United States in Central America*. New York: Norton, 1983.

La Guerre, Michael S. *American Odyssey: Haitians in New York City*. Ithaca, N.Y.: Cornell University Press, 1984.

Langley, Lester D. *The Banana Wars: United States Intervention in the Caribbean, 1898–1934*. Lexington: University of Kentucky Press, 1983.

————. *Central America—The Real Stakes: Understanding Central America Before It's Too Late*. Avenel, N.J.: Crown, 1985.

————. *The Cuban Policy of the United States: A Brief History*. New York: Wiley, 1968.

————. *The United States and the Caribbean in the Twentieth Century*. Athens, Ga.: University of Georgia Press, 1980.

————. *The U.S., Cuba, and the Cold War: American Failure or Communist Conspiracy*. Lexington, Mass.: Heath, 1970.

Lazo, Mario. *Dagger in the Heart: American Foreign Policy Failures in Cuba.* New York: Funk & Wagnalls, 1968.

León Catayo, Micanor. *Se Quiebra la esperanza?* Havana: Editora Política, 1994.

Le Reverend, Julio. *Breve historia de Cuba.* Havana: Editorial de Ciencias Sociales, 1978.

Lernoux, Penny. *Cry of the People: The Struggle for Human Rights in Latin America—The Catholic Church in Conflict with U.S. Policy.* New York: Penguin, 1980.

———. *In Banks We Trust.* New York: Doubleday, 1984.

Lettis, Richard, and William E. Morris, eds. *The Hungarian Revolt: October 23–November 4, 1956.* New York: Scribner's, 1961.

Leyburn, James Graham. *The Haitian People.* New Haven: Yale University Press, 1966.

Lieuwen, Edwin. *U.S. Policy in Latin America: A Short History.* New York: Praeger, 1965.

Lockwood, Lee. *Castro's Cuba, Cuba's Fidel.* New York: Vintage, 1967.

Lyon, Peter. *Eisenhower: Portrait of the Hero.* Boston: Little, Brown, 1974.

MacEoin, Gary, ed. *Sanctuary: A Resource Guide for Understanding and Participating in the Central American Refugees' Struggle.* San Francisco: Harper & Row, 1985.

MacGaffey, Wyatt, and Clifford Robert Barnett. *Twentieth-Century Cuba: The Background of the Castro Revolution.* New York: Doubleday, 1965.

Mallin, Jay. *Fortress Cuba: Russia's American Base.* Chicago: Regnery, 1965.

Mañach, Jorge. *Martí: El apóstol.* Madrid: Espasa-Calper, 1942.

Marchetti, Victor, and John D. Marks. *The CIA and the Cult of Intelligence.* New York: Knopf, 1974.

Martí, José. *Obras completas.* 27 vols. Havana: Editorial de Ciencias Sociales, 1975.

Masud-Piloto, Félix. "Changing Public Opinion toward Mariel Entrants: The Evolution of the Marielito Stigma." Atlanta, Georgia: Latin American Studies Association, 1994.

McCann, Thomas. *An American Company: The Gragedy of United Fruit.* New York: Crown, 1976.

McFadyen, Deirdre, and NACLA, eds. *Haiti: Dangerous Crossroads.* Boston: 1995.

Mencía, Mario. *La prisión fecunda.* Havana: Editora Política, 1980.

Menjívar, Rafael. *El Salvador: El eslabón mas pequeño.* San José, Costa Rica: Editorial Universitario Centro Americano, 1980.

———. ed. *La inversión extranjera en Centroamérica.* San José, Costa Rica: Editorial Universitario Centro Americano, 1981.

———. ed. *Revolutionary Change in Cuba.* Pittsburgh: Pittsburgh University Press, 1975.

Mesa-Lago, Carmelo. "Balseros in Limbo." *Hemisphere,* Vol. 6, No. 3: 10–13.

Meyer, Karl E., and Tad Szulc. *The Cuban Invasion: The Chronicle of a Disaster.* New York: Praeger, 1962.

Miller, Jake C. *The Plight of Haitian Refugees.* New York: Praeger, 1984.

Miller, Warren. *90 Miles From Home: The Truth From Inside Castro's Cuba.* Greenwich, Conn.: Fawcett Publications, 1961.

Millspaugh, Arthur Chester. *Haiti Under American Control, 1915–1934.* Boston: World Peace Foundation, 1931.

Munro, Dana. *Intervention and Dollar Diplomacy in the Caribbean, 1900–1921.* New York: Princeton University Press, 1964.

Nelson, Lowry. *Rural Cuba.* Minneapolis: University of Minnesota Press, 1950.

Newfarmer, Richard., ed. *From Gunboat to Diplomacy.* Baltimore: Johns Hopkins Press, 1984.

Nixon, Richard M. *Six Crises.* New York: Doubleday, 1962.

North American Congress on Latin America. *Guatemala.* New York: NACLA, 1974.

Nuñez, Jiménes, Antonio. *En marcha con Fidel.* Vol. 1, 1959. Havana: Editorial Letras Cubanas, 1982.

Oppenheimer, Andres. *Castro's Final Hour: The Secret Story behind the Coming Downfall of Communist Cuba.* New York: Simon & Schuster, 1992.

Ortiz, Fernando. *Cuban Counterpoint: Tobacco and Sugar.* Translated by Harriet de Onis. New York: Vintage Books, 1970.

Ott, Thomas O. *The Haitian Revolution, 1789–1804.* Knoxville: University of Tennessee Press, 1973.

Parkinson, F. *Latin America, The Cold War and The World Powers, 1945–1973: A Study in Diplomatic History.* Beverly Hills: Sage, 1974.

Parmet, Herbert S. *Eisenhower and the American Crusades.* New York: Macmillan, 1972.

————. *Jack: The Struggles of John F. Kennedy.* New York: Dial Press, 1980.

————. *The Presidency of John F. Kennedy.* New York: Macmillan, 1983.

Pearce, Jenny. *Under the Eagle: U.S. Intervention in Central America and the Caribbean.* Boston: South End Press, 1982.

Pérez, Louis A., Jr. *Cuba Between Empires, 1878–1902.* Pittsburgh: University of Pittsburgh Press, 1983.

————. *Intervention, Revolution, and Politics in Cuba, 1913–1921.* Pittsburgh: University of Pittsburgh Press, 1978.

Philipson, Lorrin. *Freedom Flights: Cuban Refugees Talk About Life Under Castro and How They Fled His Regime.* New York, Random House, 1980.

Phillips, David A. *The Night Watch.* New York: Atheneum, 1977.

Pierre-Charles, Gérard. *Problemas dominico-haitianos y del Caribe.* Mexico City: Universidad Nacional Autónoma de Mexico, 1978.

Plummer, Brenda Gayle. *Haiti and the United States: The Psychological Moment.* Athens, Ga.: University of Georgia Press, 1992.

Portes, Alejandro, and Alex Stepick. *City on the Edge: The Transformation of Miami.* Berkeley: University of California Press, 1993.

Portuondo del Prado, Fernando. *Historia de Cuba.* Havana, 1957.

Radvanyi, Janos. *Hungary and the Superpowers: The 1956 Revolution and Realpolitik.* Stanford: Hoover Institution Press, 1972.

Ridgeway, James, ed. *The Haiti Files: Decoding the Crisis.* Washington, D.C.: Essential Books, 1994.

Roa, Raúl. *La revolución del 30 se fue a bolina*. Havana: Editorial de Ciencias Sociales, 1979.

Robbins, Carla Anne. *The Cuban Threat*. New York: McGraw-Hill, 1983.

Rodríguez Chávez, Ernesto. "La crisis migratoria Estados Unidos–Cuba en el verano de 1994." *Cuadernos de Nuestra América*, Vol. XI, No. 22: 4–25.

Rodríguez Menéndez, Mario. *El Salvador: Una auténtica guerra civil*. San José, Costa Rica: Editorial Universitario Centroamericano, 1981.

Roig de Leuchsenring, Emilio. *Historia de la enmienda Platt*. Havana: Cultural, Sociedad Anónima, 1935.

———. *Cuba no debe su independencia a los Estados Unidos*. Havana: Editorial de Ciencias Sociales, 1950.

Rolberg, Robert I. *Haiti: The Politics of Squalor*. Boston: Houghton Mifflin, 1971.

Ronning, Neale C., ed. *Intervention in Latin America*. New York: Knopf, 1970.

Rositzke, Harry. *The C.I.A.'s Secret Operations*. New York: Readers Digest, 1977.

Rovere, Richard. *Senator Joe McCarthy*. New York: Harper & Row, 1959.

Ruíz, Leovigildo. *Diario de una traición: Cuba 1959*. Florida: Florida Typesetting of Miami Inc., 1965.

Schlesinger, Arthur M., Jr. *A Thousand Days: John F. Kennedy in the White House*. Boston: Houghton Mifflin, 1965.

Schlesinger, Stephen, and Stephen Kinzer. *Bitter Fruit: The Untold Story of the American Coup in Guatemala*. New York: Doubleday, 1982.

Schmidt, Hans. *The United States Occupation of Haiti, 1915–1934*. New Brunswick: Rutgers University Press, 1971.

Sidey, Hugh. *John F. Kennedy, President*. New York: Atheneum, 1963.

Silk, James, and Virginia Hamilton. *Despite a Generous Spirit: Denying Asylum in the United States*. Washington, D.C.: U.S. Committee for Refugees, 1986.

Smith, Earl E.T. *The Fourth Floor: An Account of the Castro Communist Revolution*. New York: Random House, 1962.

Smith, Robert F. *Background to Revolution: The Development of Modern Cuba*. New York: Knopf, 1966.

———. *The United States and Cuba: Business and Diplomacy, 1917–1960*. New Haven: College and University Press, 1960.

Sorensen, Theodore C. *Kennedy*. New York: Harper & Row, 1965.

———. *The Kennedy Legacy*. New York: Macmillan, 1969.

Suárez, Andrés. *Cuba: Castroism and Communism, 1959–1966*. Translated by Joel Carmichael and Ernst Halperin. Cambridge: MIT Press, 1967.

Suchlicki, Jaime. *University Students and Revolution in Cuba 1920–1968*. Coral Gables: University of Miami Press, 1969.

———. *Cuba: From Columbus to Castro*. New York: Scribner, 1974.

Suchlicki, Jaime, Antonio Jorge, and Damian Fernández, eds. *Cuba: Continuity and Change*. Miami: University of Miami Press, 1985.

Taber, Michael., ed. *Fidel Castro Speeches. Vol. 1, Cuba's International Foreign Policy 1975–80*. New York: Pathfinder Press, 1981.

———. *Fidel Castro Speeches. Vol. 2, Our Power Is That of the Working People: Building Socialism in Cuba.* New York: Pathfinder Press, 1983.

———. *Fidel Castro Speeches, 1984–1985. Vol. 3, War & Crisis in the Americas.* New York: Pathfinder Press, 1985.

Taber, Robert. *M-26 Biography of a Revolution.* New York: Lyle Stuart, 1961.

Tato, Robert J. *Haiti: Land of Poverty.* Washington D.C.: University Press of America, 1982.

Thomas, Hugh. *Cuba: The Pursuit of Freedom.* New York: Harper & Row, 1971.

Torres Ramírez, Blanca. *Las relaciones Cubano-Sovieticas (1959–1968).* Mexico: El Colegio de Mexico, 1971.

Torres Rivas, Edelberto., ed. *Centro América: hoy.* Mexico, D.V.: Siglo Veintiuno, 1975.

Unión de Jóvenes Comunistas. *La primera batalla de toda una generación de jóvenes.* Havana: Editora Abríl, 1980.

United Nations. *Acuerdos de el Salvador: en el camino de la paz.* New York: U.N. Department of Public Relations, 1992.

Urrutia-Lleó, Manuel. *Fidel Castro & Company, Inc.: Communist Tyranny in Cuba.* New York: Praeger, 1964.

———. *Democracia falsa y falso socialismo: Pre-castrismo y castrismo.* Union City, N.J.: Vega Publishing, 1975.

Welch, Richard E., Jr. *Response to Revolution: The United States and the Cuban Revolution, 1959–1961.* Chapel Hill: University of North Carolina Press, 1985.

Welles, Sumner. *A Time for Decision.* New York: Harper & Row, 1944.

White, Richard Alan. *The Morass: United States Intervention in Central America.* New York: Harper & Row, 1984.

White, Theodore H. *The Making of the President, 1960.* New York: Atheneum, 1961.

Wise, David, and Thomas Ross. *The Invisible Government.* New York: Random House, 1964.

Wittner, Lawrence S. *Cold War America: From Hiroshima to Watergate.* New York: Praeger, 1974.

Wood, Bryce. *The Making of the Good Neighbor Policy.* New York: Columbia University Press, 1961.

Wyden, Peter. *Bay of Pigs: The Untold Story.* New York: Simon & Schuster, 1979.

Articles, Chapters, and Pamphlets

Anderson, Jervis. "Haitians of New York." *New Yorker,* March 31, 1975, 50–55.

Appel, John. "The Unionization of Florida Cigarmakers and the Coming of the War With Spain." *Hispanic American Historical Review* 36 (February 1956): 38–49.

Areíto. "Una iglesia en Miami que apoya el levantamiento del bloqueo a Cuba." *Areíto* 3 (1979): 50–52.

Arguelles, Lourdes. "Cuban Miami: The Roots, Development, and Everyday Life of an Emigre Enclave in the United States National Security State." *Contemporary Marxism* (Summer 1982): 27–43.

Azicri, Max. "Un analysis pragmatico del diálogo entre la Cuba del interior y del exterior." *Areíto* 5 (1979): 4–7.

Bach, Robert L., Jennifer B. Bach, and Timothy Triplett. "The Flotilla Entrants: Latest and Most Controversial." *Cuban Studies* 11 (July 1981–January 1982): 29–48.

Blackburn, Robin. "The Economics of the Cuban Revolution." In Nelson Goodsell, ed., *Fidel Castro's Personal Revolution in Cuba: 1959–1973*. New York: Knopf, 1975, 133–50.

Branch, Taylor, and George Crile, III. "The Kennedy Vendetta: How the C.I.A. Waged a Silent War Against Cuba." *Harper's*, August 1975, 19–63.

Cannon, Terry. "U.S. Cuban Policy: A Future Stalled in the Past." *Cuba Review* 6 (March 1976): 19–28.

Casal, Lourdes. "Cubans in the United States: Their Impact on U.S.-Cuban Relations." In Martin Weinstein, ed., *Revolutionary Cuba in the World Arena*. Philadelphia, 1979.

———. "Fidel Castro: Invitación al diálogo." *Areíto* 5 (1979): 5–8.

———. "Cuba, Abríl-Mayo 1980: La histéria y historia." *Areíto* 6 (1980): 15–25.

Castro, Fidel. "Entrevista de Fidel con un grupo de periodistas cubanos que escriben para la comunidad cubana en el exterior y varios periodicos norteamericanos." Havana: Editorial de Ciencias Sociales, 1978.

———. "Nos enfrentamos al porvenir con la experiencia de veinte años y el entusiasmo del primer día." Havana: Editora Política, 1979.

Chicago Religious Task Force on Central America. "Basta!" Chicago, 1985.

Close, Kathryn. "Cuban Children Away From Home." *Children* 10 (1963): 1.

Coordinating Council of Dade County. "Light the Lamp." Miami: Office of the City Manager, 1980.

Copeland, Ronald. "The 1980 Cuban Crisis: Some Observations." *Journal of Refugee Resettlement* (August 1981): 22–32.

Cortada, James W. "Florida's Relations With Cuba During the Civil War." *Florida Historical Quarterly* (July 1980): 42–52.

del Castillo, Siro. "A Plea to Destigmatize Mariel." *Caribbean Review* 13 (Fall 1984): 7.

Fagen, Patricia W. "Latin American Refugees: Problems of Mass Migration and Mass Asylum." In Richard Newfarmer, ed., *From Gunboat to Diplomacy*. Baltimore: Johns Hopkins University Press, 1984.

Fagen, Richard R., and Richard A. Brody. "Cubans in Exile: A Demographic Analysis." *Social Problems* 11 (Spring 1964): 389–401.

Fox, Geoffrey. "The Cuban Exodus and the U.S. Press." *Cuba Update* 1: 4–10.

Frederick, Howard. "La guerra radial: U.S./Cuba Radio Wars." *W.I.N.*, September 1983, 9–12.

Harneker, Marta. "A Cuban Leader Answers Tough Questions." *Cuba Times* 2 (Spring 1981): 19–21.

Hedli, Douglas J. "United States Involvement or Non-Involvement in the Hungarian Revolution of 1956." *International Review of History and Political Science* 11 (1974): 72–78.

Hentoff, Nat. "Snoops in the Pews." *Progressive*, August 1985, 25–28.

Hoeffel, Paul, and Sandra Levinson. "The U.S. Blockade: A Documentary History." *Cuba in Focus* 1 (December 1979): 5–80.

Hollyday, Joyce. "A Spirit of Resolve." *Sojourners*, March 1985, 10–15.

Jones, Kirby. "Trade Winds A-Changin." *Cuba Review* (March 1976): 14–18.

Kerpen, Karen Shaw. "Those Who Left: Two Years Later." *Cuba Times* 3 (Spring 1978): 1–4.

Kirk, John M. "José Martí and the United States: A Further Interpretation." *Journal of Latin American Studies* (November 1977): 275–90.

Krajick, Kevin. "Refugees Adrift: Barred From Our Shores." *Saturday Review*, October 27, 1979, 17–19.

Lernoux, Penny. "The Miami Connection." *Nation*, February 8, 1984, 186–98.

Long, Durward. "La Resistencia: Tampa's Immigrant Labor Union." *Labor History* 6 (Fall 1965): 193–213.

———. "The Making of Modern Tampa: A City of the New South, 1885–1911." *Florida Historical Quarterly* 49 (April 1971): 333–45.

López, Alex. "Dos años en Matacumbe y Florida City: entrevista con Alex López." *Areíto* 5 (1979): 13–17.

McCaughan, Ed. "Causes of Immigration From Socialist Cuba." *Contemporary Marxism* 5 (Summer 1982): 44–47.

Morley, Morris H. "The U.S. Imperial State in Cuba 1952–1958: Policy making and Capitalist Interests." *Journal of Latin American Studies* 14 (May 1982): 143–70.

Nairn, Allan. "Assault on Sanctuary: A Church Rallies to Protect a Salvadoran Whistleblower." *Progressive*, August 1985, 20–23.

Nichols, Nick. "Castro's Revenge." *The Washington Monthly*, March 1982, 39–42.

Pérez, Louis A., Jr., "Cubans in Tampa: From Exiles to Immigrants, 1892–1901." *Florida Historical Quarterly* 57 (October 1978): 129–40.

Powers, Thomas. "Inside the Department of Dirty Tricks." *Atlantic*, August 1979, 33–64.

Payo, Gerald E. "Cuban Revolutionaries and Monroe County Reconstruction Politics, 1968–1976." *Florida Historical Quarterly* 55 (April 1977): 407–22.

———. "Key West and the Cuban Ten-Year War." *Florida Historical Quarterly* 57 (January 1979): 289–307.

Radaelli, Ana María. "Cubanos en el Peru. Dos años después." *Cuba Internacional*, September 1982, 30–33.

Rivera, Mario. "Refugee Chess: Policy by Default." *Caribbean Review* 13 (Fall 1984): 4–6, 36–39.

Rodríguez dos Santos, Luis. "The Emigrants." *Third World* 5 (1980): 18–20.

Rumbaut, Luis. "Conversación con Fidel." *Areíto* 4 (Spring 1978): 24–26, 78.

Salvadoran Humanitarian Aid, Research and Education Foundation. "El Salvador: Refugees in Crisis." San Francisco, 1982.

Schlesinger, Stephen. "How Dulles Worked the Coup d' Etat." *Nation*, October 28, 1978, 425, 439–44.

Siegel, Franklin. "Treasury Impounds Cuban Periodicals." *Cuba Times* 2 (Fall 1981): 7–9.

Smith, Wayne S. "Dateline Havana: Myopic Diplomacy." *Foreign Policy* 48 (Fall 1982): 157–74.

Snell, Moe. "Attack on Sanctuary." *In These Times*, October 2–8, 1985, 12–13.

Stepick, Alex. "The New Haitian Exodus: The Flight From Terror and Poverty." *Caribbean Review* 11 (Winter 1982): 14–17, 55–57.

Stewart, Kitty. "Welcome Back to the Free World." *Cuba Times* 5 (Fall 1984): 9–12.

Thompson, Janis R. "Haitian Refugees: Political and Historical Perspectives." Miami: United Church of Christ, 1981.

Tolan, Sandy, and Carol Ann Bassett. "Informers in the Sanctuary Movement." *Nation*, July 20–27, 1985, 40–44.

Walsh, Msgr. Bryan O. "Cuban Refugee Children." *Journal of International-American Studies and World Affairs* (1971): 378–415.

Winn, Peter. "Is the Cuban Revolution in Trouble?" *Nation*, June 7, 1980, 682–85.

Index